yes please

yes please

AMY POEHLER

DEY ST.
AN IMPRINT OF WILLIAM MORROW *PUBLISHERS*

Chapter "Don't Forget to Tip Your Waitresses" contains content first published by *The New Yorker* in "Take Your Licks," October 14, 2013.

First Dey Street mass market printing: November 2018
First Dey Street paperback printing: September 2015
First Dey Street hardcover printing: October 2014

Print Edition ISBN: 978-0-06-286784-1
Digital Edition ISBN: 978-0-06-226837-2

Designed by Headcase Design, headcasedesign.com

Cover design by Mary Schuck

14 15 16 17 18   QGM   10 9 8 7 6 5 4 3 2 1

For my bold and beautiful boys.

contents

PART ONE:

WHATEVER YOU WANT

PART TWO:

WHATEVER YOU LIKE

PART THREE:

BE

WHOEVER YOU ARE

NAME _Amy Poehler_ TEACHER _Cynthia Systrom_

GRADE _Kdg._ DATE _June, 1977_

ACADEMIC READINESS:

	ALWAYS	USUALLY	SELDOM
Completes work		✓	
Knows letters	✓		
Knows beginning sounds	✓		
Knows numbers	✓		
Counts by rote	✓		
Listens carefully	✓		
Retains information	✓		
Contributes to group	✓		

COMMENTS: Amy is an excellent student.

SOCIAL DEVELOPMENT:

	ALWAYS	USUALLY	SELDOM
Relates well to children	✓		
Relates well to adults	✓		
Shares willingly	✓		
Enjoys large group activities	✓		
Enjoys small group activities	✓		
Participates enthusiastically	✓		

COMMENTS:

writing is hard:

a preface

I LIKE HARD WORK AND I DON'T LIKE PRETENDING THINGS ARE PERFECT. I have learned that about myself. And I don't have any fear of writing. I have been writing my whole life: stories and plays and sketches and scripts and poems and jokes. Most feel alive. And fluid. Breathing organisms made better by the people who come into contact with them. But this book has nearly killed me. Because, you see, a book? A book has a cover. They call it a jacket and that jacket keeps the inside warm so that the words stay permanent and everyone can read your genius thoughts over and over again for years to come. Once a book is published it can't be changed, which is a stressful proposition for this improviser who relies on her charm. I've been told that I am "better in the room" and "prettier in person." Both these things are not helpful when writing a book. I am looking forward to a lively book-on-tape session with the hope that Kathleen Turner agrees to play me when I talk about some of my darker periods. One can dream.

It's clear to me now that I had no business agreeing to write this book. I have a job that keeps me shooting twelve hours a day, plus two children under six. I am going through a divorce and producing many projects and falling in love and trying to make appointments for cranial massage. All of these things are equally wonderful and horrible and keep me just off balance and busy enough to make spending hours alone writing seem like a terrible idea. Plus, I am forty-two, which is smack-dab in the middle. I haven't lived a full enough life to look back on, but I am too old to get by on being pithy and cute. I know enough now to know I know nothing. I am slugging away every day, just like you. But nonetheless, here we are. I've written a book. You have it.

Everyone lies about writing. They lie about how easy it is or how hard it was. They perpetuate a romantic idea that writing is some beautiful experience that takes place in an architectural room filled with leather novels and chai tea. They talk about their "morning ritual" and how they "dress for writing" and the cabin in Big Sur where they go to "be alone"—blah blah blah. No one tells the truth about writing a book. Authors pretend their stories were always shiny and perfect and just waiting to be written. The truth is, writing is this: hard and boring and occasionally great but usually not. Even I have lied about writing. I have told people that writing this book has been like brushing away dirt from a fossil. What a load of shit. It has been like hacking away at a freezer with a screwdriver.

I wrote this book after my kids went to sleep. I wrote this book on subways and on airplanes and in between setups while I shot a television show. I wrote this book from scribbled thoughts I kept in the Notes app on my iPhone and conversations I had with myself in my own head before I went to sleep. I wrote it ugly and in pieces. I tried hard not be overly dramatic, like when I wrote this poem in Social Studies class at age thirteen:

Amy Poehler

May 21, 1985
Social Studies
1:10

When life attacks you from everyside.
It hurts —
too much
And the most
painless
easiest way out is —
death
　　　　to survive.

At this very moment I am attempting to write this preface in the dark while my oldest boy, Archie, sleeps next to me. He is dreaming and talking, and I am turning down the light on the screen as I write about how hard it is to write. Writing a book is awful. It's lonely, even with Archie beside me and my editors nagging me. During this process I have written my editors e-mails with subject headings such as "How Dare You" and "This Is Never Going to Work" and "Why Are You Trying to Kill Me?" Most authors liken the struggle of writing to something mighty and macho, like wrestling a bear. Writing a book is nothing like that. It is a small, slow crawl to the finish line.

Honestly, I have moments when I don't even care if anyone reads this book. I just want to finish it.

If you are reading this, it means I have "finished." More likely, it means my editors have told me I can't keep tinkering anymore. I will take this time now to thank you for buying this and reading it and eventually turning it into a feature film with Kate Winslet/Katy Perry/Katie Couric as the star.

Let me offer this apology. Please excuse this self-indulgent preface. I know what I am doing. I am presenting a series of reasons as to why you should lower your expectations, so that you can be blown away by my sneaky insights about life and work. I am a grown woman. I know my own tricks! I know how good I am at bemoaning my process and pretending I don't care so that my final product will seem totally natural and part of my essence and not something I sweated for months and years. One of the things I have learned about me while writing about me is that I am really onto myself. I have got Amy Poehler's number, I'll tell you. I also learned that writing topless tends to relax me. Go figure. Life is a mystery.

While writing this book I made many mistakes. I kept a copy of Nora Ephron's *Heartburn* next to me as a reminder of how to be funny and truthful, and all I ended up doing was ignoring my writing and rereading *Heartburn*. I also kept a copy of Patti Smith's *Just Kids* nearby, which was awful because her writing is beautiful and poetic and how dare she. I also read and reread wonderful books by wonderful women: Rachel Dratch's *Girl Walks into a Bar . . .* , Sarah Silverman's *The Bedwetter,* Mindy Kaling's *Is Everyone Hanging Out Without Me?,* Lena Dunham's *Not That Kind of Girl,* Caitlin Moran's *How to Be a Woman,* and Tina Fey's *Bossypants*. All are superb and infuriating. My dear friend and *Parks and Recreation* cast-mate Nick Offerman had the nerve to start and publish his book *Paddle Your Own Canoe* in less time than it took me to write this preface. I congratulated him when he presented it to me and then immediately threw it in the garbage.

I made other terrible mistakes while I tried to write this book. I asked people who have already finished books for advice, which is akin to asking a mother with a four-year-old what childbirth is like. All the edges have been rounded and they have forgotten the pain. Their books are finished and in their libraries, so all they end up talking about is how you need to "stick to your guns" and "not let the editors push you around" and that "your title is important." Stick to my guns? I am hiding from my editors because I feel so guilty that I haven't worked hard enough and given them something genius or interesting or new. My title is important? Well, I am screwed, because right now I am vacillating between *The Secret 2* and *Mosquitos Love Me: A Woman's Guide to Getting Her Funk On.* The only people I can stand to read right now are Pema Chödrön, who reminds me that life is messy and everything is a dream, and Stephen King and Anne Lamott, who are two of my favorite writers on writing. But now that I think of it, both of them are funnier than me, so they can tie their sixty-eight books to their ankles and go jump in a lake.

Many people suggested ways I could carve out more time for my writing, but none of their suggestions involved the care and consideration of the small children who live in my house. Every book written by men and women with children under the age of six should have a "sleep deprived" sticker. I could find lots of discussion online about "waiting for the muse" but not enough about having to write in between T-ball games. I want more honesty from people who write books while they have small children. I want to hear from people who feel like they have no time. I remember once reading about J. K. Rowling, and how she wrote *Harry Potter* while she was a single mom struggling to make ends meet. We need to hear more stories like that. However, I do need to point out that J. K. never had to write a personal memoir AND make it funny AND do it while she had to be on camera with makeup on, AND she had ONLY ONE KID AT THE TIME IF I REMEMBER CORRECTLY. (This could be wrong; editors, please factcheck. Also let marketing know I am very interested in *Yes Please* becoming the next *Harry Potter*.)

In my desperation, I searched out other writers who were struggling and asked them if they wanted to take a break from their own misery and contribute to my book so I would have fewer pages to fill. I thought about asking Hillary Clinton but realized she was too busy writing, finishing, and publishing her own book. If I had timed it better, I could have contributed to her book and she could have contributed to mine. But I blew it. I guess my essay "Judge Judy, American Hero" will have to be read in *Harper's* at a later date.

Writing this book has been so hard I wrote a *Parks and Recreation* script in three days. It was a joy, writing in a voice that wasn't my own. I have also written two screenplays in the time it has taken me to crank this sucker out. (This isn't true but whatever. I can write a screenplay in my sleep. Shiiiiiit.)

So what do I do? What do we do? How do we move forward when we are tired and afraid? What do we do when the voice in our head is yelling that WE ARE NEVER GONNA MAKE IT? How do we drag ourselves through the muck when our brain is telling us youare-

dumbandyouwillneverfinishandnoonecaresanditis-
timeyoustop?

Well, the first thing we do is take our brain out and
put it in a drawer. Stick it somewhere and let it tantrum until it wears itself out. You may still hear the
brain and all the shitty things it is saying to you, but it
will be muffled, and just the fact that it is not in your
head anymore will make things seem clearer. And then
you just do it. You just dig in and write it. You use your
body. You lean over the computer and stretch and pace.
You write and then cook something and write some
more. You put your hand on your heart and feel it beat-
ing and decide if what you wrote feels true. You do it
because the doing of it is the thing. The doing is the
thing. The talking and worrying and thinking is not the
thing. That is what I know. Writing the book is about
writing the book.

So here we go, you and me. Because what else are
we going to do? Say no? Say no to an opportunity that
may be slightly out of our comfort zone? Quiet our
voice because we are worried it is not perfect? I believe
great people do things before they are ready. This is
America and I am allowed to have healthy self-esteem.
This book comes straight from my feisty and freckled
fingers. Know it was a battle. Blood was shed. A war
raged between my jokey and protective brain and my
squishy and tender heart. I have realized that mystery
is what keeps people away, and I've grown tired of
smoke and mirrors. I yearn for the clean, well-lighted

place. So let's peek behind the curtain and hail the others like us. The open-faced sandwiches who take risks and live big and smile with all of their teeth. These are the people I want to be around. This is the honest way I want to live and love and write.

Except when it comes to celebrities without makeup. I want my celebrities to look beautiful. I don't need to see them pumping gas.

I tried to tell the truth and be funny. What else do you want from me, you filthy animals?

I love you,

Amy

instructions for
how to use this book

THIS BOOK IS A MISSIVE FROM THE MIDDLE. It's a street-level view of my life so far. It's an attempt to speak to that feeling of being young and old at the same time. I cannot change the fact that I am an American White Woman who grew up Lower-Middle-Class and had Children after spending most of her life Acting and Doing Comedy, so if you hate any of those buzzwords you may want to bail now. Sometimes this book stays in the present, other times I try to cut myself in half and count the rings. Occasionally I think about the future, but I try to do that sparingly because it usually makes me anxious. *Yes Please* is an attempt to present an open scrapbook that includes a sense of what I am thinking and feeling right now. But mostly, let's call this book what it really is: an obvious money grab to support my notorious online shopping addiction. I have already spent the advance on fancy washcloths from Amazon, so I need this book to really sell a lot of copies or else I am in trouble. Chop-chop, people.

In this book there is a little bit of talk about the past. There is some light emotional sharing. I guess that is the "memoir" part. There is also some "advice," which varies in its levels of seriousness. Lastly, there are just "essays," which are stories that usually have a beginning and an end, but nothing is guaranteed. Sometimes these three things are mixed together, like a thick stew. I hope it is full of flavor and fills you up, but don't ask me to list all the ingredients.

I struggled with choosing a quote that would set the table for you and establish an important tone once you started reading.

I thought about Eleanor Roosevelt's "A woman is like a tea bag; you never know how strong it is until it's in hot water."

I dabbled with "A woman who doesn't wear perfume has no future" from the seemingly hilarious and real "girl's girl" Coco Chanel.

I was tempted by "I always play women I would date" from Angelina Jolie.

But Wordsworth stuck with me when he said, "Poetry is the spontaneous overflow of powerful feelings: it takes its origin from emotion recollected in tranquillity." This book is a spontaneous overflow in the middle of chaos, not tranquillity. So it's not a poem to you. It's a half poem. It's a "po." It's a Poehler po.

Wordsworth also said that the best part of a person's life is "his little, nameless, unremembered, acts of kindness and of love." I look forward to reading a book one day in which someone lists mine. I feel like I may have failed to do so. Either way, it's obvious I am currently on a Wordsworth kick and this should give you literary confidence as you read *Yes Please*.

The title *Yes Please* comes from a few different places. I like to say "Yes please" as an answer to a lot of things in my personal and professional life. The "yes" comes from my improvisational days and the opportunity that comes with youth, and the "please" comes from the wisdom of knowing that agreeing to do something usually means you aren't doing it alone.

It's called *Yes Please* because it is the constant struggle and often the right answer. Can we figure out what we want, ask for it, and stop talking? Yes please. Is being vulnerable a power position? Yes please. Am I allowed to take up space? Yes please. Would you like to be left alone? Yes please.

I love saying "yes" and I love saying "please." Saying "yes" doesn't mean I don't know how to say no, and saying "please" doesn't mean I am waiting for permission. "Yes please" sounds powerful and concise. It's a response and a request. It is not about being a good girl; it is about being a real woman. It's also a title I can tell my kids. I like when they say "Yes please" because most people are rude and nice manners are the secret keys to the universe.

And attention, men! Don't despair! There is plenty of stuff in here for you too. Since I have spent the majority of my life in rooms filled with men I feel like I know you well. I love you. I love the shit out of you. I think this book will speak to men in a bunch of different ways. I should also point out that there is a secret code in each chapter and if you figure it out it unlocks the next level and you get better weapons to fight the zombie quarterbacks on the Pegasus Bridge. So get cracking, you task-oriented monkey brains.

I still wish this book was just a compendium of searing photographs I took in Afghanistan during my years as a sexy war correspondent, but hey, there is still time.

Shall we?

part one

SAY

WHATEVER YOU WANT

"...KING OF THE FOREST..." - Steve ___ (right) delivers his lines as the ___rdly Lion, while Dorothy (Amy Poehler), ___n Man (Monica Stamm) and the Scarecrow (Brian Doherty) look on during the Wildwood School presentation of "The W___ Oz."

(Rick Karw___

how i fell in love with improv:

boston

I WAS IN FOURTH GRADE AND IN TROUBLE. The students of Wildwood Elementary School in Burlington, Massachusetts, shifted in their uncomfortable metal seats as they waited for me to say my next line. A dog rested in my arms and an entire musical rested on my shoulders. I was playing Dorothy in *The Wizard of Oz,* and it was my turn to speak. Dorothy is *Hamlet* for girls. Next to Annie in *Annie* and Sandy in *Grease,* it is the dream role of every ten-year-old. Annie taught me that orphanages were a blast and being rich is the only thing that matters. *Grease* taught me being in a gang is nonstop fun and you need to dress sexier to have any chance of keeping a guy interested. But *The Wizard of Oz* was the ultimate. It dealt with friendship and fear and death and rainbows and sparkly red shoes.

Up to this moment, I had only been onstage twice. The first was for a winter pageant in second grade. I was dressed as a snowflake and had to recite a poem. The microphone was tilted too high, and so I stood on my tiptoes and fixed it. A year later I was in a school play in the role of a singing lion. My "lion's mane" (a dyed string mop worn on my head) kept slipping, and I surreptitiously adjusted it midsong.

My parents would later point to these two small moments and tell me that was when they knew I would be a performer. Honestly, I don't think I had a burning desire to act at that young age. Back then, I didn't know acting was a job, really. All I knew was I liked roller-skating in my driveway and making people sit and watch. I liked setting up dance contests in my basement and being the only judge. I liked attention. Attention and control. Attention, control, and, it turns out, laughs.

In *The Wizard of Oz,* the part of Dorothy isn't exactly the comedic lead. She spends a lot of time listening to other people explain themselves. She is the straight man among a bunch of much juicier character parts. The Wicked Witch of the West is more dynamic. The Scarecrow has a bigger arc. Even the Lollipop Guild has a killer song. Dorothy just asks a lot of questions and is always the last to know. I didn't care. At the time, I was in fourth grade, which, for me, was a heavenly time to be a girl. It was all elbows and angles and possibility. I hadn't gotten my period or kissed a boy. My beloved grandfather hadn't yet died of a heart attack on my front porch on the Fourth of July. I wanted to be an astronaut or a scientist or a veterinarian and all signs pointed to my making any or all of that happen. The worst things I had encountered to this point were lice (which I'd had), scoliosis (which I didn't), and the threat of nuclear war (a shadow that loomed over everything). My generation was obsessed with scoliosis. Judy Blume dedicated an entire novel to it. At least once a month we would line up in the gym, lift our shirts, and bend over, while some creepy old doctor ran his finger up and down our spines. Nuclear war was a high-concept threat, two words that often rang out in political speeches or on the six o'clock news. Our spines. Lice. Nuclear war. The Big Three.

AIDS was just around the corner, but we didn't know it yet. The only AIDS I knew were Ayds, an unfortunately named caramel diet candy my mom had in our kitchen cabinet. The anxiety-filled eighties would dovetail nicely with my hormonal teenage years, but in fourth grade, in 1980, I felt like I would live forever.

I stood onstage in my blue-checked dress, Toto in my arms, and looked at the audience of parents, teachers, and students. I breathed in and had a huge realization. I could decide right then and there what the next moment would be. I could try something new. I could go off script and give something a shot. I could say *whatever* I wanted.

It was because of this Dorothy Moment that I had the nerve, years later, to try out for the high school musical. It was my senior year and Burlington High School had been a great place for a floater like me. I weaved in and out of activities and groups, and hid on occasion. My school was big and sprawling, with four hundred students in my graduating class. I played basketball and soccer for a while and I thought I might be some kind of athlete. My dad was a semipro basketball player in college and I inherited his hand-eye coordination. I was a decent point guard and middling fullback. Softball was the most fun because of the opportunity to shit-talk. But my enthusiasm for team sports fell away once I realized I would never be great. (Once they move you from shortstop to second base, you might want to start making other plans.) I was a cheerleader for a while. I did student council. I started to hang with the popular crowd but was never considered the prettiest or most interesting. I tended to blend. In my high school yearbook I was voted third runner-up for "Most Casual." I never figured out if that meant most casual in dress or in overall manner. In any case, I didn't come in first. I guess the two ahead of me wanted it less.

Every year our school put on one musical, and in my senior year I auditioned for *Once Upon a Mattress*. I didn't know any of the "theater kids" by name. My experience with musicals was limited, at best. In our sophomore year, my class had taken a trip to New York City and gone to a few Broadway shows. We saw a production of *The Fantasticks*, which I liked, and *A Chorus Line*, which I loved. The part of Diana Morales spoke to me. I loved that she was short and blue-collar. I loved how she stood up to her grumpy and withholding acting teacher, Mr. Karp. I loved how she cried when that bastard died. Because she FELT NOTHING. So badass!

On the same trip, we visited the Empire State Building and the World Trade Center, as well as swinging by 30 Rockefeller Center and taking the *SNL* studio tour. We pressed our noses against the glass and watched the *SNL* cast rehearse. It was 1985, and Anthony Michael Hall and Robert Downey Jr. were on the main stage. I would meet both of them twenty years later—I directed Anthony Michael Hall in a reenactment of *Sixteen Candles* for a VH1 program, and I met Robert Downey Jr. in a Hollywood coffee shop, where I pitched him my idea for a little indie film called *Iron Man.*

In *Once Upon a Mattress,* I was cast as Princess Winnifred, a part that had physical set pieces and lots of loud singing. It would be the beginning of me playing a long line of crazy big-mouths.

Carol Burnett had originated this role on Broadway and I loooooved *The Carol Burnett Show.* I loved Carol Burnett. She was funny and versatile and up for anything, but most importantly, I could tell that the ensemble around her loved her. I could tell that she was a benevolent captain of that team and was having a hell of a time. Watching that show proved that good comedy can be fun and you don't have to treat people badly to be on top. I felt the same when I watched Gilda Radner, Andrea Martin, and Catherine O'Hara. You could tell that the cast adored them. You could see Bill Murray look at Gilda in a way that told you he loved her, for real.

I was lucky enough to meet and do an interview with Carol Burnett once, for *TV Guide*. I told her that I loved everything about that show: how it represented time spent with my mother, how it reminded me of myself as a young woman learning to love comedy, how when she took off her makeup and answered questions at the end of the show it was such a generous act because she seemed like one of us. She said, and I quote, "Oh, Amy, you are my new best friend!" It's in print, I swear.

A lot of people ask me if I always knew I was going to be on *Saturday Night Live*. I think the simple answer is: yes. I don't mean to sound cocky. I didn't know if I had the talent or drive, I just had a tiny little voice whispering inside of me. That same voice would tell me I would meet Carol Burnett someday, I would find love, I would be okay. We all have a tiny whispery voice inside of us, but the bad ones are usually at a lower register and come through a little clearer. I don't know where the good voice came from. It was a mix of loving parents, luck, and me. But ever since I was a small child, I would look at places where I wanted to be and believe I would eventually be on the other side of the glass. I believed that someday in the future, I would be rehearsing onstage at *Saturday Night Live* while a gaggle of sophomore girls would be waving to me. All of them wearing cooler outfits than my classmates and I wore that day.

My high school musical did not offer a shirtless Zac Efron, but it did provide me with many lessons. I learned that I loved being in a theater, attending rehearsals, and building sets. I loved listening to the director and groaning about rehearsing choreography. When I would leave the bright sunlight of outside and enter into the dark and empty theater, I would feel like a real artist with a true sense of purpose. Time passed and the world spun, but all that mattered was the thing in the room you were making together. I started to go to theater parties and tried cigarettes. I had floated into the right pool, finally.

The play itself went well, from what I remember. It was a blur of adrenaline and costume changes. I reveled in this new feeling of being incredibly stressed and pulling things off last-minute. (A talent that I hope will help me finish this goddamn book—dear lord, when will I finish this book?) My parents rushed to congratulate me after the show. "You were so great, Ames!" my mom said. "You don't have to go to college if you don't want to!" my dad exclaimed. My mother hit him in the arm and told him he was crazy. This one-two punch of support and realism would help me deal with the many years of rejection I didn't know were ahead of me. I then thought about the idea of being an actress and tried it on for size.

Back to fourth grade, *The Wizard of Oz* and Dorothy. I stood onstage in soft Dearfoams slippers. My mother had bought two pairs at Bradlee's, and we spray-painted them silver and sparkly red. My hair was braided and I was wearing my own denim overall dress and blue-checked blouse. It was my time to speak during the tornado scene. All of the other actors were supposed to be running around and reacting to heavy winds. A teacher made a whistling-wind sound effect on a handheld microphone and construction-paper tumbleweeds were rolled across the stage. In my arms was Toto, played by a real dog. Some sucker had allowed us to cast their tiny poodle as Toto, which in hindsight begs the question: What kind of maniac hands over their tiny dog to a bunch of ten-year-olds for an elementary school play?

We were in the second night of a blistering two-night run. The previous evening I had delivered my line "Toto, Toto! Where are you?" during the tornado scene. The problem was the damn dog was in my arms at the time. The audience laughed. Lightning struck— and I discovered three important things. I liked getting a laugh. I wanted to get one again. But I wanted to get it in a different way and be in charge of how I got it. So, I stood onstage that second night and tried something new.

Trying something new was all I wanted to do when I graduated high school. I was so excited to go to Boston College that I distinctly remember wiggling in my seat as I wore my cap and gown. I wanted to go, go, go. Arriving at Boston College was like moving to a new country. I was unprepared for the fact that most of the kids were a lot wealthier than me. I met prep school kids who knew how to decorate their rooms with tapestries. I became friends with private school athletes who were familiar with living away from home. I studied with foreign students who had their own credit cards. When I got the name of my new freshman roommate sent to me in the mail, I noticed she was from Illinois and so I immediately assumed she lived on a farm. I was wrong. We spoke on the phone and I asked her if classical music was playing in the background and she informed me that was the sound of her doorbell. Her name was Erin and she ended up being very nice and fun. We would sing the soundtrack to *Les Misérables* by the light of a neon beer sign her dad sent us to put in our dorm room window.

I looked at my high hair and heard my New England accent and realized I was certainly bringing a lot of Boston to my Boston College experience. I decided I might want to tone both my hair and the lazy r's down a little. The accent is a really hard thing for me. It reminds me of my family and my childhood, but it's one of the worst-sounding accents out there. I love Boston, but we sound like idiots. Our mouths never close and we talk like big, lazy babies. I might get shit for this but as a true Bostonian all I will say to that is

FUCK YOU, AHHSOLE, IF YOU GOT A PRAWBLEM
WIT ME THEN LET'S MEET BY THE RIVAH!

During my first week of freshman orientation I
went to a performance at the Eagles Nest, the BC cafeteria and general social center. I was struck by how
much fun it looked. It was ensemble comedy. It was
improvisation. It was quick jokes and group mind
dynamics. Everyone was getting to act and be funny
and write and direct and edit all at the same time. The
group was called My Mother's Fleabag and it was the
oldest running improvisational group on campus. I
wanted in. I met Kara McNamara, one of the performers. She was a Boston girl and would eventually be my
roommate, and she pushed me to audition, though I
have no memory of actually doing it. I think it was
mostly short-form improvisational games. I do remember that it was thrilling. I went back to my room and
waited.

We were told that we made the group by being
woken up in the middle of the night and taken to a
secret location to drink. It was like being hazed for one
day, which is the exact amount of hazing I am able to
withstand. We rehearsed constantly. We would spend
hours arguing over one joke. Relationships were
formed and trust was built. My Mother's Fleabag per-
formed shows a couple of times a year. A cover band
played "Pulling Mussels (from the Shell)" by Squeeze,
and we would run out in baseball shirts. We did

short-form improv games, sketches, and songs based on specific Boston College humor. It was fun but not too cool, and it got me in front of an audience. I had a theater I went to every day and a group that needed me all the time. It was heaven.

Kara and I moved in with a bunch of men and women off campus and my college life sort of exploded in happiness. We used to host big and boozy parties. We had a "Good-bye to the Eighties" party and everyone dressed in costume. At least twenty different women arrived in sexy Robert Palmer–girl outfits. I dressed as Baby Jessica, the little girl who fell down the well. (And was successfully rescued! Important fact!) I wore pajamas and pigtails and made my face a little dirty. Sexy stuff. We lived on a street called Strathmore and our motto was "Live More, Love More, Strath More." I learned about Charles Busch and Kate Bush. I sat with the cool Jesuit priests and talked about Edna St. Vincent Millay. I took classes like "The Medium Is the Message" and "The Male Lens." I carved out a pretty groovy off-campus curriculum in what was a very competitive academic program. I spent my days directing scenes from *True West* and my nights writing sketches about bad cafeteria food. I studied Shakespeare and learned to control my voice, and at night I huddled with a bunch of misfits and practiced being stupid on purpose.

I didn't really know what kind of actor I wanted to be back then. I didn't have a real plan or even a mentor to follow. I just knew the things I didn't want. I didn't want to be tied down and stuck. I didn't want to decide who I was going to marry or where I was going to live. I took a public speaking class in college with Craig Finn, a friend of my cousin Lynn (Sheehan) Gosselin. Craig is a great musician who is now the lead singer of the band Hold Steady. I remember feeling like we both knew a secret: we were going to keep performing no matter what, and we both were going to have no money, stability, or children for the next ten years. I think we should stop asking people in their twenties what they "want to do" and start asking them what they don't want to do. Instead of asking students to "declare their major" we should ask students to "list what they will do anything to avoid." It just makes a lot more sense.

I was in my off-campus Strathmore kitchen when Kara told me she was going to move to Chicago after she graduated. She was a year ahead of me and had heard about these classes at the comedy mecca Second City. Further investigation led us to research ImprovOlympic, and they also had classes. That settled it. Kara was going to Chicago and was going to get an apartment, and I would join her a year later. "I can be a waitress anywhere!" I said to my horrified parents, who had remortgaged their small house twice to pay for my brother and me to go to college.

I started to believe in myself. I realized I could say whatever I wanted.

In the second and final performance of *The Wizard*

of Oz, I decided to take control during the tornado scene. I paused, put the blinking dog down on the stage, and walked a few feet away from it. "Toto, Toto! Where are you?" I said, pretending to look for my lost dog in the fearsome storm. The dog froze and played it perfectly. I got laughter and some light applause for my efforts. I had improvised and it had worked. One could argue that it worked because of the dog. A good straight dog can really help sell a joke. Whatever. I have been chasing that high ever since.

plain girl
vs.
the demon

I HATE HOW I LOOK. That is the mantra we repeat over and over again. Sometimes we whisper it quietly and other times we shout it out loud in front of a mirror. I hate how I look. I hate how my face looks my body looks I am too fat or too skinny or too tall or too wide or my legs are too stupid and my face is too smiley or my teeth are dumb and my nose is serious and my stomach is being so lame. Then we think, "I am so ungrateful. I have arms and legs and I can walk and I have strong nail beds and I am alive and I am so selfish and I have to read *Man's Search for Meaning* again and call my parents and volunteer more and reduce my carbon footprint and why am I such a self-obsessed ugly asshole no wonder I hate how I look! I hate how I *am*!"

There have been forty million books and billions

of words written on this subject, so I will assume we are all caught up.

That voice that talks badly to you is a demon voice. This very patient and determined demon shows up in your bedroom one day and refuses to leave. You are six or twelve or fifteen and you look in the mirror and you hear a voice so awful and mean that it takes your breath away. It tells you that you are fat and ugly and you don't deserve love. And the scary part is the demon is your own voice. But it doesn't sound like you. It sounds like a strangled and seductive version of you. Think Darth Vader or an angry Lauren Bacall. The good news is there are ways to make it stop talking. The bad news is it never goes away. If you are lucky, you can live a life where the demon is generally forgotten, relegated to a back shelf in a closet next to your old field hockey equipment. You may even have days or years when you think the demon is gone. But it is not. It is sitting very quietly, waiting for you.

This motherfucker is patient.

It says, "Take your time."

It says, "Go fall in love and exercise and surround yourself with people who make you feel beautiful."

It says, "Don't worry, I'll wait."

And then one day, you go through a breakup or you can't lose your baby weight or you look at your reflection in a soup spoon and that slimy bugger is back. It moves its sour mouth up to your ear and reminds you that you are fat and ugly and don't deserve love.

This demon is some Stephen King from-the-sewer devil-level shit.

I had a lucky childhood. My demon didn't live in my room. My demon just walked around my neighborhood. I grew up with a naturally pretty but very earthy mother who never told me to put on makeup or change my outfit. I didn't have the kind of mother who flirted with my friends or wore tight jeans.

In middle school I was small and flat chested, which was also a lucky break. You can kind of slip around unnoticed that way, which is exactly what you want. I was made fun of for being short, but it was mostly by boys who were shorter than me. I rarely brushed my hair and I was skinny. I bordered on being a tomboy, but not enough to be labeled one. It was a wonderful but short-lived time when I was in my body but not critical of it. If you ever want to see heaven, watch a bunch of young girls play. They are all sweat and skinned knees. Energy and open faces. My demon would receive my school picture and maybe gently suggest I "do something about those eyebrows," but for the most part it left me alone. I felt safe in the middle—a girl who had a perfectly fine face but not one that drew any attention.

Then I started caring about boys and the demon pulled into my driveway.

The eighties were a strange time for teenage fashion. We wore silk blouses and shoulder pads, neon earrings and jodhpur pants. Come to think of it, our pants were especially weird. We also wore stirrup pants, parachute pants, and velvet knickers. It was a real experimental pant time. We curled our hair and sprayed it until it was crunchy and high. We wore jewel tones and too much makeup. With the exception of a few naturally beautiful girls who knew how to balance all of these elements, we looked ridiculous.

Dating in middle school often meant walking around the mall together and spending hours on the phone picking "your song." There was light hand-holding and maybe a kiss on the cheek, but it was really all very innocent. I "dated" one boy and our song was "Faithfully" by Journey. Every time it played my body would turn electric, and I would stare out whatever window I was near and reminisce about experiences I hadn't had. Is there a word for when you are young and pretending to have lived and loved a thousand lives? Is there a German word for that? Seems like there should be. Let's say it is *Schaufenfrieglasploit*.

Dating in high school was very different. Boys suddenly went up your shirt. Girls were expected to give blow jobs and be sexy. You had to be hot but not a slut. You had to be into sex but never have it, except when your boyfriend wanted it. If you had sex you had to keep it a secret but also be very good at it, except not too good, because this better be your first time. Darling Nikki masturbated to a magazine, but Madonna was supposedly still a virgin. It was very confusing. Once high school started, I began to see the real difference between the plain and the pretty. Boys, who were going through their own battles started to point out things about me I hadn't yet noticed. One told me I looked like a frog. Some told me I smiled like a Muppet. A senior told me to stop looking at him with my "big, weird eyes." I looked in the mirror at my flat chest and my freckles and heard a sound. It was the demon, suitcase in hand. He moved in and demanded the top bunk.

Now, as I continue, please know a few things. I usually find any discussion about my own looks to be incredibly boring. I can only imagine what a yawn fest it is for you. But I cannot, in good faith, pretend I have fallen in love with how I look. The demon still visits me often. I wish I could tell you that being on

television or having a nice picture in a magazine suddenly washes all of those thoughts away, but it really
doesn't. I wish I were taller or had leaner hands and a
less crazy smile. I don't like my legs, especially. I used
to have a terrific flat stomach but now it's kind of
blown out after two giant babies used it as a short-
term apartment. My nose is great. My tits are better
than ever. I like my giant eyes, but they can get crazy.
My ass is pretty sweet. My hair is too thin for my lik-
ing. My Irish and English heritage and my early sun
exposure guarantee that I am on the fast track to wrin-
kle city.

Bored yet? Because I can't stop.

I went through high school and college and the
years after dating all different types of people. I think
if you lined them up in a row there would not be one
single physical characteristic that they all shared.
Most were white. Not all. Some were short and hairy,
some were weird, some pretty, sweet, athletic. I would
say that maybe most of the men I dated had a small
current of anger fueling them, but that is the case for
most funny people. I dated a lot of really funny people.
And some medium funny. The best-looking ones were
medium funny at best—it's tough to be both. In Chicago I dated a "male model" for a hot minute. It was
the first time I had dated someone that "handsome"
but the truth was he was in my improv class and not
that funny, so I felt weirdly superior.

I made the mistake of snooping and reading the

model's journal. We finished having medium-to-boring sex and I rifled through his things while he took a shower. I am pretty good at snooping around. It started in my own house, where I would go through every drawer and every pocket in my parents' room. Luckily, I didn't find much at home except for some well-worn copies of *Playboy* that seem positively charming compared to the up-close butt fisting that pops up on my computer these days when I am trying to order salad tongs from Target. I honed my snooping skills when I babysat. It was then that I saw my first diaphragm, laxatives, and stacks of cash in an underwear drawer. I have basically ransacked every house I have been allowed into. My snooping tendencies have now abated somewhat, but I still have to fight the urge to immediately go through people's shit. I am not proud of this and I realize that by admitting this I am limiting future opportunities to be a houseguest.

Anyway, the bad part about snooping is you can find stuff you don't want to find. Snooping in e-mails, texts, or journals is a disaster. No one says good things about people in diaries. You tell people the good things. Diaries are for the bad things! I found an entry from model man that basically said he was kind of proud of himself for dating someone like me. He thought I was "funny but not that pretty, which was kind of like cool, you know?" He, like, wasn't "into me but like was totally down for the journey." Like, cool, man. I remember thinking, "HA HA! I know that already, dummy. We just had boring sex and I win because I tricked you with my personality! I don't even like you!"

Then I went home and cried and took way too long to break up with him.

But I was eventually okay. And you will be okay too. Here's why. I had already made a decision early on that I would be a plain girl with tons of personality, and accepting it made everything a lot easier. If you are lucky, there is a moment in your life when you have some say as to what your currency is going to be. I decided early on it was not going to be my looks. I have spent a lifetime coming to terms with this idea and I would say I am about 15 to 20 percent there. Which I think is great progress. I am not underestimating the access I get as a BLOND, WHITE lady from AMERICA. Believe me, blond hair can take you really far, especially with the older men. It can really distract from the face. I am convinced I could have had sex with both Tony Bennett and John McCain if we weren't each happily married at the time we all met.

Decide what your currency is early. Let go of what you will never have. People who do this are happier and sexier.

Being considered beautiful can be tough. I know this because I work in Hollywood, which is filled with the most conventionally beautiful people in the world. Beautiful people can get objectified and underestimated. They didn't do anything to earn their genes so they have to struggle to prove they are more than their hot bods. People assume they are happy and good in bed, and most times this is not true. Plus, some beautiful people get a little addicted to being told they are beautiful and have real trouble when they get older, get less attention, or have their spouse cheat on them with someone considered "plain."

Improvisation and sketch comedy helped me find my currency. My plain face was a perfect canvas to be other people. There is nothing I like more than picking out wardrobe for a character. An *SNL* hairstylist once told me I had a great face for wigs. A Great Face for Wigs! What a compliment. (And also the title of my second book.) Looking silly can be very powerful. People who are committing and taking risks become the king and queen of my prom. People are their most beautiful when they are laughing, crying, dancing, playing, telling the truth, and being chased in a fun way.

Improvisation and sketch comedy let me choose who I wanted to be. I didn't audition to play the sexy girl, I just played her. I got to cast myself. I cast myself as sexy girls, old men, rock stars, millionaire perverts, and rodeo clowns. I played werewolves and Italian prostitutes and bitchy cheerleaders. I was never too this or not enough that. Every week on *SNL* I had the opportunity to write whatever I wanted. And then I was allowed to read it! And people had to listen! And once in a blue moon it got on TV! And maybe five times it was something really good. Writing gave me an incredible amount of power, and my currency became what I wrote and said and did.

If you write a scene for yourself you can say in the stage directions, "THE MOST BEAUTIFUL WOMAN IN THE WORLD ENTERS THE BAR AND ALL THE MEN AND WOMEN TURN THEIR HEADS." Then you can write a scene where you say, "SERGIO, THE MOST GORGEOUS MAN WE HAVE EVER SEEN, STARTS TO KISS HER." If you are lucky enough to be directing this scene you can have casting sessions and bring in various attractive men and see if they are good at kissing you. You will arrive on set and the call sheet at the start of your day can read, "JASMINE HAS SEX WITH SERGIO IN A ROWBOAT," and then you can go have fake sex with someone and still not cheat on anybody. Men do this all the time. Acting isn't all bad.

Hopefully as you get older, you start to learn how to live with your demon. It's hard at first. Some people give their demon so much room that there is no space in their head or bed for love. They feed their demon and it gets really strong and then it makes them stay in abusive relationships or starve their beautiful bodies. But sometimes, you get a little older and get a little bored of the demon. Through good therapy and friends and self-love you can practice treating the demon like a hacky, annoying cousin. Maybe a day even comes when you are getting dressed for a fancy event and it whispers, "You aren't pretty," and you go, "I know, I know, now let me find my earrings." Sometimes you say, "Demon, I promise you I will let you remind me of my ugliness, but right now I am having hot sex so I will check in later."

Other times I take a more direct approach. When the demon starts to slither my way and say bad shit about me I turn around and say, "Hey. Cool it. Amy is my friend. Don't talk about her like that." Sticking up for ourselves in the same way we would one of our friends is a hard but satisfying thing to do. Sometimes it works.

Even demons gotta sleep.

PLASTIC
SURGERY
HAIKU

If you plump your lips
The words that come out of them
Sound ridiculous

We know it's Botox
And not your vegan diet
Nice try, Margaret

A face-lift does not
Make daughters comfortable
When you chaperone

Fine, get your boobs done
But only make them smaller
Fake boobs are weird, y'all

Asymmetrical
Looks cool while cheek implants are
Less interesting

Plastic surgery
Requires a good amount
Of lying to friends

Can I be honest?
You look like a lady from
The Broadway show *Cats*

I have no idea
If you are angry or sad
Since you got fillers

Hey, shooting poison
In your face does not keep you
From turning fifty

laughing to crying
to laughing

DOING SKETCH COMEDY ON LIVE TELE-
VISION WHILE PREGNANT IS LIKE WEARING
A SOMBRERO. You can pretend to be a serious
person, but the giant hat gives you away. I have spent
an inordinate amount of time on camera being pregnant. Sometimes it was real and sometimes it was not.
When I shot the film *Baby Mama* I wore a fake belly. It
was shaped like a watermelon cut in half and it was
strapped onto my body with flesh-colored Velcro. I
would adjust it to where it felt comfortable and then
giggle at the sight of it under my clothes. I would rip
my belly off at lunch and the satisfying Velcro rip
would announce that my pregnancy was over. Many
times I patted my sweaty and firm stomach and
thought about how cool it was going to be when I really
was pregnant.

Real pregnancy is different.

I always wanted to have kids. I like them. They

like me. I'm a mother now and I think I am pretty good at it. I think I am a decent person and very good listener and excellent at funny faces, all necessary when mothering a child. When I was twenty-six, a Japanese healer felt my abdomen and told me I had a joyful uterus and I would have three children. He worked in a dusty office that smelled like envelope glue. He gave me a bunch of herbs to help with my anxiety, which is why I was actually there, but when I boiled the herbs the smell was so horrible that I became instantly anxious at the thought of ingesting them and threw them in the garbage. In addition to my joyful uterus, I have what my nana referred to as her "Irish stomach." This means that when I get old I should limit myself to buttered saltine crackers and the occasional hot dog. I associate hot dogs with the very young and the very old. Once after a grueling rehearsal at *SNL* for a Mother's Day show (where I was six months pregnant with my second son) I asked the indefatigable Betty White what she was going to do when she got home. She told me she was going to fix herself a "vodka on the rocks and eat a cold hot dog." In one sentence, she proved my theory and made me excited for my future.

Most of my thirties were spent married and without children, which is a state of affairs that I would highly recommend most people try for a while. Married and without children means you can go on vacations with other childless couples. You can eat in any restaurant at any time and have conversations about interesting things. You can decide to learn how to surf or write a slim book on the best place to buy a fedora in Los Angeles, because your spouse will be supportive and no one has to go home to relieve the babysitter. I was in no rush to change this wonderful lifestyle. Then I woke up and realized I was thirty-seven and might need to get cracking.

Pregnancy is such a sensitive and subjective experience. Trying to get pregnant is the most vulnerable thing in the world. You have to openly decide you are ready and then you have to put sperm in your vagina and elevate your legs like you are an upside-down coffee table. It's all ridiculous and incredibly sci-fi. Everyone's journey is different and I have nothing to say about how and when someone decides to become a mother. The legacy of my generation will be that we have truly expanded the idea of what "family" means. It is no longer unusual for people who choose surrogacy, gay adoption, IVF, international and domestic adoption, fostering, and childlessness to live side by side and quietly judge each other. We can all live in peace thinking our way is the best way and everything else is cuckoo. I was lucky. I tried for a little while to get pregnant, and at thirty-seven I did.

I didn't tell anyone at first, as you are supposed to keep it secret. It's a really magical time, those first few weeks. It almost makes you wish you didn't have to tell anyone, ever. You could just watch your belly grow bigger and no one would be allowed to ask you about it and you would have your baby and a year later you would allow visitors to finally come and meet your little miracle. I was halfway through my seventh season at *SNL*, and no one really noticed my nausea or extreme tiredness. That was par for the course at a job that made you stay up all night long and eat cold mozzarella sticks you had to buy yourself.

My ob-gyn was a wonderfully old Italian man I will call Dr. G. Dr. G had delivered Sophia Loren's children. I know this because everyone from his receptionist to the other doctors in his practice liked to tell me this fact. I was happy to hear that Dr. G was comfortable with beautiful and famous vaginas. I don't consider myself beautiful or famous, but my vagina certainly is. Everyone knows this. I have the Angelina Jolie of vaginas. And there is your pull quote, editors.

"I have the Angelina Jolie of vaginas."

But even with my glamorous vagina, I worried about delivery. I have many friends who have had natural childbirth. I applaud them. I have friends who have used doulas and birthing balls and pushed out babies in tubs and taxicabs. I have a friend who had two babies at home! In bed! Her name is Maya Rudolph! She is a goddamn baby champion and she pushed her cuties out *Little House on the Prairie* style!

Good for her! Not for me.

That is the motto women should constantly repeat over and over again. Good for her! Not for me. I knew early on that my big-headed babies were going to be tricky to get out of my five-foot-two-inch frame. I knew that I was worried about pain and wanted to have the right measures in place. I knew I was the kind of person who could barely go to the movies without being stoned, let alone a delivery room. I remember a very important day when I told my dentist I wanted nitrous oxide at the ready every time I came for an appointment. No matter the procedure. No questions asked. This is what adults do. They demand or deny drugs on their own terms. Luckily, Dr. G made me feel like I would be able to handle anything.

Dr. G was European and old-fashioned in all the right ways. He reassured me I didn't need an amniocentesis by reminding me that Italian women don't worry about that sort of thing. I imagined Sophia Loren laughing off the idea of a needle being driven into her pregnant belly as she sipped an espresso. Dr. G dressed in stylish suits and moved very gently, squirting cold gel on my tummy while whistling a slow tune. He didn't have a 3-D imaging machine. He had a utilitarian black-and-white deal that showed you a blurry picture of what looked like a big-headed frog. "Your baby is very smart," he would say to me and my husband, Will Arnett. "You are doing everything right. Please drink one or two glasses of red wine a night."

I was so lucky to have Dr. G as my doctor. I didn't feel neurotic or stressed. I felt like a success. I ate what I wanted and felt super sexy. I was lucid enough to realize that I was on a total hormonal high and that a crash was just around the corner, but I didn't care. I loved being pregnant. I loved being at work and still feeling vital and busy while this extraordinary thing was happening inside me. I never felt alone. I always had a companion. I reveled in all the new space I was taking up. When your stomach is big you knock things over and everyone stays out of your path. I was big in brand-new ways and I felt very powerful and womanly.

I couldn't have chosen a better doctor to deliver my first child. Unfortunately that never happened. Dr. G died the day before I went into labor.

Yup.

But before I get to that . . .

The last week of *SNL* before my son Archie arrived was incredibly exciting. The 2008 presidential race was almost a dead heat and the entire year leading up to the election had been a magical time to work on a live satirical sketch comedy show. Everything felt electric. The audience knew the ins and outs of every political story, and a lot of it had to do with what *Saturday Night Live* was doing. I think everyone was crushing it that season and the show had never been better.

We could barely keep up with the daily goodies and produced four prime-time *Weekend Update Thurs-*

day specials during September and October. I was eight months pregnant and did fifteen live shows in thirteen weeks. Everyone came on. I met then presidential candidate Barack Obama while I was dressed as Dennis Kucinich. Maya was dressed as Barack Obama at the time, so the introduction might have been slightly more embarrassing for her. We were doing a sketch about how hot Kucinich's wife was. That's how much America was paying attention! Then Tina played Sarah Palin for the first time and blew the roof off the joint.

The anticipation of Tina playing Palin was so fun to witness, and she explains it well in her book *Fifty Shades of Grey*. She totally took on what was expected of her and it was awesome to stand next to her as she killed. The sketch that night dealt with Hillary Clinton coming to terms with the possibility of a Vice President Sarah Palin. It dealt with fierce competitiveness in politics. It dealt with power and entitlement. It dealt with the way society forces women to define themselves and compete against each other. It tackled old theories about Madonna vs. Whore and Slut vs. Shrew. But most importantly, it was really funny. That sketch was written by Seth Meyers. Tina and I added jokes. *SNL* and now *Late Show with Seth Meyers* producer Mike Shoemaker wrote the legendary line "I can see Russia from my house."

I remember standing onstage and it being one of the few times that something felt perfectly whole. Archie did flips in my stomach each time the audience clapped. It was the closest to what I imagine it feels like to write a hit song. Here is a picture of Shoemaker and Seth rehearsing that skit with us. Look how in love with us they are.

My stomach grew bigger and the election grew closer. With just a few weeks left, Governor Sarah Palin was asked to come on the show. I had never met her, but many years before I had met Senator John McCain when he hosted and liked him instantly. We did a scene in a shower together and he was totally appropriate while also being very pleased. He was vigorous and honest. He noticed me smoking and told me if he knew the world was going to end the first thing he would do is start smoking again. He invited me to his house in Arizona. We hit it off.

I knew Tina would do a great opening sketch with Sarah Palin, and Seth and I were trying to think of something to do with her at the "Update" desk. I think I made some kind of joke about getting her to do a hard-core rap or something. Then I laughed at the thought of my doing one near her, in the gigantic state I was in. Seth laughed too. It was certainly not some wildly original idea, but as usual at *SNL*, the time pressure let us do things without overthinking. When you are pregnant you can get away with a lot of shit. Women really are at their most dangerous during this time. Your hormones are telling you that you are strong and sexy, everyone is scared of you, and you have a built-in sidekick who might come out at any minute. There should be some kind of pregnancy superhero movie. Calling Hollywood now. What's that, Hollywood? It's a weird idea and also you don't do movies with female super-heroes? Copy that.

I went into my dressing room and wrote the rap. Seth helped. Andy Samberg helped. I met Palin in her dressing room beforehand to go over things and I was honestly surprised that they didn't make us change more of it. She and her team only wanted to modify a small joke about Todd being a real ladies' man, I think. Her daughter Bristol was pregnant at the time, and we made small talk about babies. I did the rap and it was super fun. My stomach looked so big it almost seemed fake. It was ridiculous. I was so tired between dress and air that I remember lying in my dressing room like a bear and sleeping deeply in between sketches.

Which brings us to Friday, October 24, 2008. The

day I went into labor. The day after my doctor died. The musical guest that week was Coldplay, and it was going to be Jon Hamm's first time hosting the show. I had been working the whole time and feeling pretty good. Exhausted, yes. But invigorated. And honestly, at the end of a pregnancy any lady will tell you she is searching for anything to take her mind off the creature that is about to burst forth.

So I had done my rap the previous Saturday and slept all day Sunday feeling happy. Will and I had our suitcases packed and a name picked out. We were both so happy and so in love. Nothing brings a couple closer than a baby about to arrive. Each person needs the other so desperately and in such new and deep ways. Each day through the week, I was doing my check-in with the doctor. As we all know, a watched cervix never dilates, and I'd still been tight and sassy that Thursday morning. Dr. G assured me I would probably deliver a few days late like most new mothers. I told him that I was doing the show on Saturday, even though it was technically my due date, but any time after that would be fine. It was the first of many times I ridiculously thought I had any control over my schedule, this baby, or life and death in general.

I was in the middle of rehearsing a *Mad Men* parody Friday morning and called to confirm my three P.M. appointment. The receptionist answered the phone crying. She told me Dr. G had passed away from a heart attack in his sleep. I burst into tears so loudly and violently that I think water was squirting out of my eyes like in a *Cathy* cartoon. Nothing is more horrifying than a giant pregnant lady sobbing. Everyone got very quiet. I hung up the phone and told Jon and the hair and makeup people that my doctor had just DIED. And I was DUE TOMORROW. And that I knew it seemed like a weird punch line, but my beloved and dear Italian grandpa was not going to be able to help me. I felt so terrible about the fact that all I was thinking was "What about meeeeeee!" I cried and cried in my *Mad Men* dress. Jon Hamm held me by the shoulders and looked at me and said, "I know this is very sad, but this is a really important show for me, so I'm going to need you to get your shit together." This made me laugh so hard I think I peed. Going from crying to laughing that fast and hard happens maybe five times in your life and that extreme right turn is the reason why we are alive, and I believe it extends our life by many years.

I told everyone at dress rehearsal. It freaked them out. At three P.M. I went to Dr. G's office and was met by his grieving colleagues who had worked with him for decades. One of them, the lovely Dr. B, examined me and told me I shouldn't worry. Nothing was happening and I would probably deliver a few days late. He had already treated and met with Dr. G's other patients and would spend the next twenty-four hours delivering five babies. He was kind and professional, but it was extremely weird. He was a stranger. I went back to *SNL,* where I stayed until two A.M. Maya and Fred Armisen were doing bits on the main stage pretending to be robot versions of themselves, and I laughed and laughed and for the millionth time thought about how lucky I was. Eddie the security guard walked me to the car and asked me how I was doing. "I'm tired," I said. I went home and got in bed. It was three thirty in the morning and I put on my favorite TV show, *Law & Order*, to go to sleep. I heard the "bam bam" sound effect in the opening credits and my water broke.

Did you know that when your water breaks the best thing to do is stand up? Your baby acts like a plug. Isn't that insane? Strange thoughts like this and others filled my head as Will and I tenderly got ready to go to the hospital. I had that nervy feeling you get when you know your whole life is going to change and you realize you're made of tissue paper. Will raced around and I weirdly brushed my teeth. As we got our car from the garage our doorman predicted we were going to have a girl. I sat down in Will's car and gushed all over it. I was worried that he would be upset, but he laughed as he helped me in. I looked at him and thought, "I've turned into an animal now and I have a feeling this will be the nicest thing you see all night."

I took drugs and pushed. It was hard and long. I texted Shoemaker and Seth and told them I wouldn't be coming to work. While I tried to get my little bugger out, *SNL* scrambled to replace my parts. The real

Elisabeth Moss came in to play herself, and she met Fred Armisen, who one year later to the day would become her husband. I would go to their wedding on my one-year-old boy Archie's birthday. Seth Meyers prepared to do "Update" alone for the first time. He would go on to do it alone successfully for years, although I like to think it was a tiny bit less fun. My big-headed wonder couldn't get out, and I started to think crazy thoughts. What if this was the one baby they couldn't get out? What if they just handed me back my clothes and sent me home and said, "We are so sorry, we did what we could but we just couldn't get him out. We wish you the best." I felt like the bouncer of my own uterus. I was ready to turn on all the lights and kick that baby out. "Time to wrap it up. I don't care where you go but you can't stay here."

I finally had a C-section. As I was wheeled into the operating room one of the nurses said, "Hey, it's Hillary Clinton!" and I answered by barfing all over her. Full circle.

Archie was born Saturday, October 25, at 6:09 P.M., just about when we would have been getting ready to do our first run-through for "Weekend Update." He was, and remains, perfect. My whole world cracked open and has thankfully never been the same since. I watched *Saturday Night Live* that night, drugged to the gills. I watched scenes that I had rehearsed hours before. I watched Maya and Kenan sing a song to me, and Seth tap my spot at the "Update" desk and tell me they loved me. I cried and cried and then laughed and laughed. I added a few more years to my life. I kissed Archie's giant head, which was shaped like a beautiful balloon. Today we wear the same size sombrero. He is six.

HELLO, EVERYONE. MY NAME IS SETH MEYERS and I will be writing this next chapter so that Amy can take a break. It is very hard to write a book. I haven't written one myself but I know it's very hard because every time I have seen Amy in the past year she has greeted me by saying, "Hello," quickly followed by, "It is very hard to write a book." At one of these meet-ups I offered to write a chapter for her so she could rest. She said, "Yes please." After I complete this favor for Amy I will only owe her one thousand more favors. I am not unique in my great debt to her. Most of Amy's friends owe her around one thousand favors. She never holds it over you though. She's not that kind of person.

I'm going to write about the night that Amy gave birth to her first son, Archie.

Before I get there, a bit of background. I first saw Amy Poehler perform in Chicago at a theater called ImprovOlympic in the midnineties. That theater is now called "iO" because the Olympics threatened to sue. The International Olympic Committee was worried people would walk into a one-hundred-seat theater on the corner of Clark and Addison and wonder why no one was jumping over hurdles.

The night I first saw Amy, she and the other performers were playing an improv game called "The Dream." She asked for a volunteer to come onstage and tell her about their day. I raised my hand and she picked me. My first conversation with Amy was in front of an audience: me in a chair, her standing beside me. She was charming, funny, sweet, and sharp, and I left thinking, "I would like to be her friend."

The next time I saw Amy perform was with Tina Fey in the same theater. They were workshopping a show called *Women of Color*. I would learn later that it was the only performance of that show. Amy would move to New York soon after and Tina would quickly follow. There weren't a lot of people in the audience that night and for a while I thought seeing Amy and Tina perform in Chicago right before they left and got famous would be the most interesting thing that ever happened to me. In my mind it was like seeing the Beatles in Hamburg. And much, I'm sure, like someone who saw the Beatles in Hamburg, I talked about it so much that my friends eventually said, "*Genug*."

At this point, my relationship to Amy was the same as everyone else's. I was a fan.

I auditioned for *SNL* in 2001. My manager called me to tell me I had been hired. He then listed the other new cast members, one of whom was Amy. My first thought after hanging up the phone wasn't "Oh my god, I'm going to be on *SNL*," it was "Oh my god, I might get to be friends with Amy Poehler."

I am happy to say we were friends right away.

I won't bore you with the details of our many years of friendship and collaboration on the show for no other reason than it is likely Amy has dedicated dozens of pages to that topic in this very book. I wouldn't be surprised if a photo of me graces the cover of this book. To take up any more time talking about it would be redundant.

Instead I will pick up the action years later on the Saturday before the Saturday Amy became a mother. Josh Brolin was hosting the show that week, but this fact would soon be rendered a footnote when Sarah Palin agreed to do a cameo.

In 2008, under intense pressure from the comedians' lobby, Senator John McCain selected Alaska governor Sarah Palin as his running mate. This brought much good fortune to *SNL* in the form of Tina Fey's mimicry. However, the fact that Governor Palin would actually be appearing on the show was not immediately greeted with cheers.

It wasn't that we weren't excited to have her on; we just didn't know what to do with her once she got there. When you perform a sketch about a person when they're not in the room you have a great deal more freedom than when they are in the room. It was understood that we'd have to write a sketch with Tina and the governor, and we did. It was a soup of moving parts; Alec Baldwin, Lorne, and Mark Wahlberg made cameos, there were some jokes, and it went well.

Sensing that the audience might want more, on Friday night Lorne suggested using Governor Palin a second time, on "Weekend Update." We sat in our weekly joke read kicking around ideas that failed to inspire any enthusiasm. For a laugh, someone said the governor could do a rap, perhaps starting with the line "I'm Sarah Palin and I'm here to say . . ." Someone else suggested that the governor could get cold feet and Amy could do the rap instead. I don't remember if either of these ideas was meant to be real but I do remember that Amy's eyes went wide with glee and she left the room with a notebook in hand. The next time I saw her she was on the phone with the wardrobe department barking orders like mission control trying to get a shuttle back. "I need Eskimo suits for Fred and Andy, a snowmobile suit for Jason, and a moose suit for Bobby."

Take a second here. Go back and watch the Palin Rap one more time. Maybe you forgot how convincing and believable Sarah Palin was when she said she wasn't going to do the piece; maybe you forgot exactly how pregnant Amy was when she stood up from behind the desk; you probably remember that Amy was good but you likely forgot exactly *how* good. It is a performance without artifice. She's not play-rapping. She's rapping. I still get goose bumps when I think of Amy screaming, "I'm an animal and I'm bigger than you!" And the whole time she was doing it, for every single second of it, there was a little person sloshing (that's the correct medical term, yes? Sloshing?) around in her belly.

That person, Archie, is getting older every day,

and soon he will be aware enough to watch and appreciate what his mother was doing on national television the week before he was born. When I want to smile, I think of that.

A week later, on the Friday before the Saturday that Amy became a mother, the entire cast stayed late to block a sketch called "The Barack Obama Variety Half Hour." On a normal week, the last piece rehearsed was usually a smaller piece with a handful of cast members cursing their luck that they had to stay at the studio until eleven P.M. the night before a show. This time, having everyone there together was a luxury and a delight.

While we waited for the cameras to set up, Maya and Fred started a bit pretending they were onstage for the seventy-fifth anniversary of *SNL*. Moving slowly and speaking softly, they delighted us with wooden award-show banter wherein they tried to remember the lines to their old sketches. Bill Hader took the stage pretending to be his own son and gave a speech about how much his "pops" had talked about working on the show before he died.

We were all enjoying ourselves that night, but no one more than Amy. She was laughing the hardest but that wasn't surprising. In my time at *SNL* no one was quicker or more gracious with a laugh than Amy—never more so than at the weekly table read, when it was needed most. When a new cast member or writer had a piece bombing to such silence that you could almost hear their pores expelling sweat, you could always count on Amy to give them a laugh. Though to be fair, it was less a laugh and more of a cackle. The writer Alex Baze described it as the sound one hears when running over a raven's foot with a shopping cart. It is, without exaggeration, one of my favorite sounds on earth.

We all headed home around midnight, in a great mood.

A quick but necessary tangent: For years Amy has called me "Coco" and I have called her "Moses." These nicknames sprung from a "Weekend Update" joke about a six-foot-tall camel named Moses and his tiny pony sidekick, Coco, who had escaped from a zoo in Texas. I don't remember the joke but I do remember that we laughed every time we said "a six-foot-tall camel named Moses and his tiny pony sidekick, Coco."

At three A.M. or so on Saturday morning Amy texted me. "Water broke, Coco! You're gonna do great!"

And that text is pretty much all you need to know about Amy. Instead of focusing on any of her fear, her excitement, or the anticipation that comes with giving birth for the first time, she sent *me* words of encouragement. And when I went out to do "Update" without her I was glad she had. I was nervous and lonely but I remembered that "You're gonna do great!" and felt better. Amy is rarely wrong.

Doing comedy for a living is, in a lot of ways, like a pony and a camel trying to escape from the zoo. It's a ridiculous endeavor and has a low probability of success, but most importantly, it is way easier if you're with a friend.

So that's my chapter. I am going to shake Amy awake now so she can continue with the hard work of writing a book for all of us. I hope she got some rest!

BIRTHING PLAN

To all Caregivers, Doctors,
Obstetrical Fellows, TMZ Interns,
and Hospital Staff:

We are looking forward to the birth of our child and
ask that the following wishes be respected during
our birth process.

We have chosen to give birth in a hospital because
of the outstanding facilities it makes available
to us. We would also like to deliver our baby in a
hospital since we spent most of our twenties getting
stoned and watching episodes of *ER*, and so we
know that delivering a baby is the best way to cheer
up an attractive but beleaguered doctor. Please
make sure our doctor is handsome and "cares too
much." We considered a home birth, but we just got
our hardwood floors redone. We also considered a
birthing tub, but the mother is concerned the water
won't be warm enough. Is it too late to flood the
hospital room? Or turn it into a really fun foam

party? We are sorry for asking. The mother is very pregnant and would like to remind everyone her brain has turned into spaghetti.

Those we plan to have present at our birth include: Baby, Mother, Father, Grandparents, Lawyers, Agents, Lottery Winners, Lookie-Loos, Midwife, First Wife, Life Coach, Finnoula the Doula, Unexpected Ghosts, Bossy Astrologist, and the entire cast of *Cheers*. All other visitors and unnecessary staff may be turned away, unless they are wearing something cute. Or bring hot wings for the father.

The birth environment is very important to us. For that reason we ask that the lights be kept dim, noise be avoided, and the door be closed for privacy. We would also like people to stay "chill" and not "bring their own shit" into the room with them. It's really important we feel "cool." Please decorate the room with Nan Goldin prints and leather beanbag chairs. We would love it if you could bring in a silk Persian rug for us to destroy. Think Chateau Marmont if it was closed for repairs. Or the set of *MTV Unplugged*.

Speaking of music, we will arrive with our own. We plan on delivering our baby to the soundtrack of Pink Floyd's *The Wall* while simultaneously watching *The Wizard of Oz*. If this kid works with us, we guarantee your minds will be blown!

The mother will wear her own clothes to the birth. If the delivery is on "Casual Friday," the mother will be wearing a tube top and bike shorts. Regardless of the day, the father will be in a fun tuxedo with jokey suspenders. Both the parents are in entertainment and have no business wear to speak of. Everyone else should be wearing open hospital gowns with nothing underneath. It only seems fair.

We plan on handling pain in a variety of natural ways. Please have a birthing ball and back massager available upon request. An annoying nurse with an unfunny and teasing manner on whom we can focus our anger would be a welcome addition. The mother would also like a punching bag, a screaming pillow, a mirror to smash, and a small handgun. The father would like a George Foreman grill, just to have.

We ask for vaginal exams only upon request. The mother requires at least a minute or two of chitchat before cold fingers are introduced. The mother would like to remind the staff that her vagina is the absolute last thing that she wants to have touched right now. The mother can think of a thousand things that she would rather have presently poked at than her vagina. Honestly, the mother doesn't know how the hell that baby is going to get out of there. The mother also would like to request that the handsome doctor maintain eye contact at all times during said poking.

If induction becomes necessary, we are aware of the nonchemical methods and would like to try them in this order: breast stimulation, sexual intercourse, and cervical cream. That's right, you heard us. If this baby isn't coming out, we are going to start doing it and make you all watch. So, let's get cracking.

We will use the squatting or semi-squatting position for pushing. Preferably the mother would like to "drop it like it's hot." The mother would like to push at her own pace. The father would like to add that he hopes it doesn't "take all day." We would like to feel our son's head as he descends with the option to stick him back up in there if we don't feel ready. The mother should be given the freedom to walk around during labor. Light choreography is expected.

If drugs become necessary, we would like to go all in. We are talking epidural, helium, and roofies. The mother would like to ask one last time why no one is taking seriously her request for nitrous oxide. The mother heard about women in England and Sweden and Canada being offered this at birth and apparently it works wonderfully to calm nerves and help with delivery. The mother still resents the judgment she received from doctors and friends when she brought up this idea. Either way, if drugs have to be administered, both mother and father know a guy.

If delivery assistance is needed, we prefer "suction" over "forceps." If episiotomy is needed, we prefer "buttonhole" over "backstitch." If cesarean is needed, please inform us early so we don't have to go through the above first.

In the event of a cesarean, the mother would like to be conscious. The mother would also not mind if you tweaked her abs while you're down there. The father would like to be present and totally freaked out when he accidentally looks past the curtain and sees his wife's organs stacked next to her like laundry.

The father would like to be involved in the "catching" of the baby and the "cutting" of the cord. At least that's what he is saying right now. We'll see. Please don't cut the cord until it stops pulsing. Please immediately let the cord blood guy in with

his titanium suitcase so he can put the cord blood
in a vault and keep it fresh. It will help us during
the robot apocalypse.

After birth we wish to nurse immediately. Please
do not introduce formula or bottles or pacifiers
or water, unless those things stop this baby from
crying. Why won't he stop crying? Wait, where is
everybody going?

We prefer our stay in the hospital to be extended to
the longest period our insurance will allow. We need
time for our heads to catch up with our bodies. We
also need to catch up on some *Judge Judy*. Please
know we are grateful and sore and happy and
scared. We will hear our baby down the hall and
recognize his cry and we will realize this truly is
a sci-fi miracle sent to us from G-O-D.

That being said, if people buy gifts that aren't on
the registry the mother will lose her shit.

The mother would like to take this moment to
admit a few things. She thinks natural childbirth is
amazing but she also likes drugs. She didn't put
baby oil on her perineum and try to stretch it
because she just never felt like it. She lied when
she said she completely stayed away from lunch
meat. She also skipped Lamaze because sometimes

she can't stand being around other people. That's all. We good?

Thank you in advance for your support of our choices. We look forward to a wonderful birth. We are excited but mostly scared. Have you SEEN the mother? She is TINY! How is this going to WORK exactly? Please advise.

the day i was born

I REMEMBER MANY DETAILS ABOUT THE DAYS MY SONS CAME INTO THE WORLD BUT VERY LITTLE ABOUT MY OWN BIRTHDAY. Partly because I was a newborn baby, and partly because my mother was always a little coy about how the birth went down. When people celebrate birthdays I like to have them describe the day they were born. Sometimes it's fun to see if the birth matches the personality. Does a big baby turn into a big adult? Does a baby born at home turn into a homebody? Does a baby born on New Year's Eve end up being a real party monster?

I was born September 16, 1971, in Newton, Massachusetts. The most popular song at the time was "Joy to the World" by Three Dog Night. *All in the Family* had been on for less than a year, Evel Knievel had just set a world record jumping over nineteen cars, and Disney World would open a month later. My mother was twenty-four years old and my father was about to turn twenty-five, and they had been married for a short eleven months. Mom wore yarn in her hair and claims she doesn't remember a thing about labor. Back then there was this wonderful thing called "twilight sleep" where women were given anesthesia at the onset of labor and woke up with a baby. Today "twilight sleep" is when you pass out on your bed while looking at paparazzi photos of Robert Pattinson eating an omelet. I always pictured my mom in a deep sleep, her beautiful thick hair (that I didn't inherit) spread out like a fan on the pillow. *The Best of Bread* played on the radio while some doctor pulled me out using groovy seventies fondue forks. I figure now would be a good time to ask her how that day went down.

T WAS 1971, THE AGE OF ALMOST "UNNATURAL CHILD-BIRTH." I had no childbirth education classes, no prenatal diagnostic tests, no ultrasound. I started labor and Dad took me to the hospital. He went home to await the birth at Nana and Gunka's house. There was no push to include fathers in the delivery room at the time, so that didn't feel strange.

I didn't feel afraid. My contractions stalled, so they had to break my water. Things moved pretty fast from then on. I remember the pain, being administered a "saddle block" anesthetic, and then helpful nurses and my doctor encouraging me at the moment of birth. You were slight in weight but unusually long, making for an easy delivery.

I was thrilled to have a daughter. My mother had modeled so successfully how to bring up daughters. I can still remember that first rush of motherly pride, that assurance that my child was perfect, and then that first twinge of self-doubt. Was I ready for this job? I look like a kid in the pictures, with a long ponytail, smiling and probably overly confident. Right after you were born, you were happily bottle-fed and then returned to the nursery and I was given four days in the hospital to recuperate. It all seems so separate and sterile now, so different from today's emphasis on instant mother-child bonding. Yet I felt great and it had all gone so smoothly.

Pregnancy had been a different story. I was sick almost every day up to your birth, sometimes on the way to work. I was teaching third grade in a nearby elementary school in 1971 and the policy was that I was supposed to resign my job upon finding out I was pregnant. An understanding principal looked the other way and I made it through the school year. Over the summer, I gave up my job in preparation for stay-at-home motherhood. There were virtually no other options available. My parents were still young and working full-time. There was no day-care facility nearby. For me, it just wasn't socially acceptable to go back to work full-time and I had always followed the rules. I was the oldest daughter in my family, the one who was working her nine-to-five shift at the bra department in our local store while her sister was at Woodstock. I studied, graduated, got a job, fell in love, got married, and had a baby. I left my job to take care of my daughter. That's the way things were done. That's the way all of my friends were doing it.

We moved away to a not-so-neighboring town. Dad went to work every day with the car and you and I were alone all day, in unknown territory. No one knew about postpartum depression then, or dared to speak its name ("Snap out of it!" was the more common reply), but knowing what I know now, I am quite sure that the signs were there for me. I was often overcome with loneliness, unsure about my choices, missing my friends. Motherhood was a twenty-four-hour-a-day, all-encompassing job. It was the hardest job I had ever had. Everything that happened to you happened to me. I had once heard children described in a novel as "hostages to fortune" and certainly my happiness depended on yours. You were not a sleeping baby. You stared at me with those blue eyes at all hours of the day and night.

I would walk the length and breadth of our town, singing Helen Reddy's "You and Me Against the World." It was the time of the burgeoning women's movement and the National Organization for Women had just been launched, and I was curious and bewildered at the same time. Where did I belong in this new world?

Moving to a new suburban town when you were five made all the difference. Here lived some college friends and a host of other educated women. Most of them were also at home providing full-time child care. These women and I "volunteered" and you came with me. We made paths for a town walking trail, read to kindergartners, delivered meals to shut-ins, and constructed floats for the Fourth of July parade on which you and your brother sat proudly and waved. We were busy and productive, involved in town politics and issues. It was the beginning of networking for me, a time of making connections and defining goals and career plans. You were always part of all this, watching me become my own person, motivated and ready for change.

—EILEEN POEHLER

I **WAS THRILLED TO HAVE A DAUGHTER AND SPE-CIFICALLY** asked the florist to put a card on the arrangement that read, "Glad it's a girl!" I have never forgotten holding you as a newborn, with your whole fanny fitting in the palm of my hand. I figured I would wait for the appropriate time to describe this to you, and now seems like a nice, private moment!

—BILL POEHLER,
also chiming in

That's my birth story. I was small and fussy, and remain so as an adult. Three years later my younger brother and only sibling, Greg, was born. I remember my father dressing me to go to the hospital and my mother commenting on how he put the wrong pants on me. I remember loving my brother instantly. He was my first friend.

If your parents are still alive, call them today and ask them to describe the day you were born. Write the details down here, on the following pages. Tell the story every year on your birthday until you know it by heart.

The Day I Was Born

_____

_____

_____

_____

_____

_____

_____

_____

_____

_____

_____

_____

_____

sorry, sorry, sorry

I SAY "SORRY" A LOT. When I am running late. When I am navigating the streets of New York. When I interrupt someone. I say, "Sorry, sorry, sorry," in one long stream. The sentence becomes "Sorrysorrysorry" and it's said really fast, as if even the act of apologizing is something to apologize for. But this doesn't mean I am a pushover. It doesn't mean I am afraid of conflict or don't know how to stand up for myself. I am getting to a place right in the middle where I feel good about exactly how much I apologize. It takes years as a woman to unlearn what you have been taught to be sorry for. It takes years to find your voice and seize your real estate.

I am still learning the right balance. Sometimes I go too far the other way. I have a quick temper and I'm not afraid to argue. Once, I was flying from New York to Toronto with Tina Fey and Ana Gasteyer on our way to shoot *Mean Girls*. We were flying in first class and spent the hour-long, ten A.M. flight chatting about life and work. The man sitting next to me was in an expensive suit on his way to a meeting, and I got the sense that he hated us and our friendly back-and-forth. A few times during the flight he sighed loudly, which I took as a sign that we were bothering him. I ignored it. Maybe that was a mistake, but sighing doesn't really work on me. As we got off the airplane and headed toward the moving walkway, the man pushed past me and jostled me a bit.

"Excuse me," I said.

"Excuse me? Excuse you!" he said.

I looked up at his boring, rich-guy face. He was turning red. I realized he was preparing to scold me. He had bumped into me on purpose to teach me a lesson.

"You girls were talking the entire flight," he said. "You should not be in first class!"

All of my lower-middle-class Boston issues rose to the surface. I don't like it when bratty, privileged old white guys speak to me like I am their mouthy niece. I got that amazing feeling you get when you know you are going to lose it in the best, most self-righteous way. I just leaned back and yelled, "FUUUUUUUUUUUCK YOU." Then I chased him as he tried to get away from me.

"You rich motherfucker! Who do you think you are? You're not better than me. Fuck you and your fucking opinions, you piece of shit."

And on and on. Tina was laughing. Or horrified. I don't remember; I was in a rage haze. Also I was show-ing off, which can be at the very least embarrassingly transparent and at the very worst careless and danger-ous. But who doesn't love self-righteous anger? It's great. When I yell at the dads drinking coffee and looking at their phones at the playground while their seven-year-olds play on the preschool monkey bars, I feel like I am fully alive.

But for the most part I try not to yell "fuck you." I try to say "yes please." And "thank you." "Yes please" and "thank you" and "sorry, sorry, sorry."

But there was one "sorry" that I took too long to say, and it haunted me for years.

Saturdays at *SNL* were a tornado of activity. I would typically be in eight or nine sketches a night, which meant fast costume changes and lots to prepare. Costume changes at *Saturday Night Live* are a dance all to themselves. Each week I would confab with my human pit crew and figure out how much time I had to change between sketches. I would change under bleachers and tucked away in corners. Hearing the sound of the audience while I was in my underwear was thrilling and terrifying. My job was to stay still and obey directions as they were shouted: "Lift your foot!" "Snap this shut!" "Close your eyes!" Bruce would pull off my pre-Velcroed shirt as Robert glued on my fake mustache. I would hold up my two index fingers next to my head while Jeffrey put on my old-man wig, and Spivey would stand next to me telling me that my new cue to enter was "Thanksgiving is ruined!" Everyone was equal during those moments, all of us actors in a play trying to get changed in time. I watched Robert De Niro wiggle into spandex pants as Siegfried. Or Roy. I witnessed Donald Trump stepping into a chicken suit. I engaged in small talk with Derek Jeter as he was buttoned into a dress. "How are you doing?" I asked. "Are you nervous?" He just laughed and said, "No," thus settling the long-standing debate about what is more nerve-racking: live comedy or the World Series.

"*SNL* time" is completely different from real-world time. Gena, our stage manager, would peek in and reassure us that we still had "a minute twenty." Our shoulders would relax and we would joke around like emergency room doctors. We would chat about someone's boyfriend as we hustled to the stage floor, and more than once a prop was thrown to me with seconds to go. I would catch it, the crowd would clap, and the scene would start. It was chaos. It was so exciting.

The problem with busy shows is that details get lost. Attention is not equally paid and things slip through the cracks. It was in one of those cracks that I did the only sketch I regret from *SNL*. The crack is not an excuse. Or maybe it is. This essay is about apologies, and I have learned an important part of apologizing is not making excuses. But that night was particularly busy.

It was March 2008 and I was newly and secretly pregnant. I remember feeling tired and worn out. Hillary Clinton was in the cold open and I stood beside her wearing a matching outfit. It's always extremely weird to play someone as they stand next to you. Coming down from that much adrenaline can drain you. Later that night, I played Dakota Fanning, hosting *The Dakota Fanning Talk Show*. I don't do an impression of Dakota Fanning, or look anything like her, so the sketch depended on my creepy ability to play a ten-year-old girl with relative ease. It was written by two *SNL* writers who liked the idea of a highly intellectual Dakota Fanning discussing things that were far too mature for her young age. Her references were often lost on her beleaguered bandleader, Reggie, played by the always-brilliant Kenan Thompson. Dakota would confess that she was a big fan of Vonnegut but "not familiar" with Harry Potter. She loved Tom Waits and enjoyed discussing Japanese poetry. She treated her mom like her manager and claimed she never watched TV. Her upcoming projects were always serious and much too adult. You get the idea.

On this particular night, the awesome Ellen Page was the host. Ellen was playing a young and innocent Miley Cyrus. This was in the *Hannah Montana* days, and Miley/Ellen was showing Dakota her new doll. The script read like this:

ELLEN/MILEY

Hey Dakota, check this out! It's my new
Hannah Montana doll! Pretty awesome, right?

(ELLEN TAKES OUT A CUTE DOLL AND MAKES IT DANCE)

AMY/DAKOTA

I've also got a new doll. It's from my

upcoming film *Hurricane Mary*, where my sister
and I play severely disabled twins.

(AMY/DAKOTA TAKES OUT A CREEPY DOLL)

ELLEN/MILEY

(AS HER DOLL)

Hey Dakota, want to play?

AMY/DAKOTA

(AS HER DOLL)

I wish I could but I am severely disabled.

I rehearsed the sketch and went over the blocking.
The entire time I assumed that *Hurricane Mary* was
something the writers had made up. We did a run-
through and I was told the doll was being made and
would be ready by air. The night of the show came, and
the doll arrived. As it was put into my hands, I remember feeling my stomach tighten. It had been manipu-
lated to look like a strange and twisted girl. But there
was no time. Jeffrey adjusted my wig. Gena told me I
had five seconds. The scene played fine. I ran to the
next quick change. Robert glued on a beard. I forgot
about my weird feeling, finished the show, and went to
the after-party.

Months later I received a letter from Marianne
Leone and Chris Cooper. It was simple and painful. It
said something like "Shame on you for making fun of a

real girl. Her name is Anastasia and she is amazing. You should know her story." I knew Chris Cooper from his work in films like *American Beauty* and *Adaptation*. I had always heard he was a wonderful person and a delight to work with. I didn't know his wife, Marianne, but a quick Google search told me a few important things: Marianne was an actor and had written the television movie *Hurricane Mary* mentioned in our skit. *Hurricane Mary* was based on the real story of Alba and Anastasia Somoza, twin sisters with cerebral palsy, and their mother's battle to ensure their right to an equal-opportunity education, as well as their full integration into society. Marianne and Chris had come to know Anastasia's story through their advocacy for disabled children. The cause was personal for them: their beloved son, Jesse, had been born with special needs. Sadly, he had passed away in 2005.

I'd like to tell you that I responded to the note. Or that I turned around and faced that letter head-on. I'd even like to tell you that I checked my body and heart and realized I was fine with the sketch and felt no need to apologize. Nope. Instead, I got angry. Anger and embarrassment are often neighbors. Sometimes we get defensive about what we feel guilty about. I was angry about the fact that I was being accused of something I didn't do. I didn't make fun of a real girl on purpose! I would never do that! That's not me! That's not me at all! I reread the note over and over again. I shared it with other people in the hopes they would agree that Marianne and Chris were overreacting and I was right to believe I was a good person. I told everyone about it and asked everyone to say it wasn't my fault. I threw the note in the trash like it was evidence of a crime. I stomped around for a bit and then pretended it went away. I was a shitty version of myself. The shadow side. I made a lot of noise because I felt bad about hurting someone's feelings and I didn't want to get quiet and really figure out how I felt. I was afraid to lie down and put my hand on my heart and hear the tiny voice whispering inside me saying that I had screwed up.

Your brain is not your friend when you need to apologize. Your brain and your ego and your intellect all remind you of the "facts." I kept telling myself that the only thing I was guilty of was not paying attention. Sure, I was being self-absorbed and insensitive, but who isn't? Sure, I should have been more on top of what I was saying, but wasn't that somebody else's job? Didn't everyone know how busy I was? Didn't Marianne and Chris take into consideration what a NICE PERSON I was? My brain shouted these things loud and clear. My heart quietly told a different story.

Shame is difficult. It's a weapon and a signal. It can paralyze or motivate. My friend Louis CK likes to say that "guilt is an intersection." Getting out of it means making a choice and moving forward. I felt guilty and I felt shame, but I didn't really move. For years. I parked my car in the intersection and let it sit there until the battery ran out. Then Spike Jonze helped me.

I bet you didn't expect so many A-list names in my apology story!

A word about apologizing: It's hard to do it without digging yourself in deeper. It's also scary and that's why we avoid the pain. We want so badly to plead our case and tell our story. The bad news is that everybody has a story. Everyone has a version of how things went down and how they participated. It's hard to untangle facts and feelings. For me, as a person in comedy, I am constantly weighing what I feel comfortable saying. There are big differences between what you say on live television and what you say at dinner, but you realize you have to be responsible for all of it. Each performer has to figure out what feels right. I am a strong believer in free speech and have spent most of my adult life in writers' rooms. I have a high tolerance for touchy subject matter. There isn't a taboo topic I can think of that I haven't joked about or laughed at. But I have an inner barometer that has helped me get better at pinpointing what works for me and what feels too mean or too lazy. I like picking fair targets. I don't like calling babies on websites ugly or comedy that relies on humiliation. I love ensembles and hate when someone bails or sells their partner out. I love watching a good roast but don't think I would be particularly good at roasting someone. Maybe it all comes down to what you feel you are good at. I have a dirty mouth but know that I don't always score when I work really blue. I have a sense of what kind of jokes I can get away with and still feel like my side of the street is clean. I like to lean my shoulder against limits and not depend on stuff that is shocking.

That being said, I still made a joke about someone being disabled. I didn't know it was a real person, but why does that matter? All of this left me stuck in that guilt intersection. I knew I was wrong but couldn't move. I lived in fear of running into Chris and Marianne, which was strange, because there really wasn't anyone else in the world I was afraid to be in a room with. This made famous-person stuff stressful, because Chris was famous and an actor and there was a high chance I would run into him at an award show.

I don't want to back-door brag as I make my way to the end of this apology tale, so let me just front-door brag and talk about the cool people I get to be friends with. I am friends with Kathleen Hanna and Adam Horovitz, aka Ad-Rock from the Beastie Boys. I can't believe I am friends with them. I love Kathleen's music and I am in awe of her social activism and general awesomeness. I asked her to interview me for *Interview* magazine when I was just a sketch performer whom nobody knew. She said yes because she supports young women. This is the artist who pulled women to the front at her rock shows. She shows up and does the work and is the real deal. Now she is my friend. Her husband, Adam, is also my friend. I used to listen to the Beastie Boys on my Walkman and dream about meeting them. Now I have Adam's e-mail. I'm blowing my cool cover but I am so psyched we are friends. I am also friends with Spike Jonze. Guess who else I am friends with? Kim Gordon! Norman Lear! Martin Short! It's awesome! I can't lie, it's so awesome!

See how I am trying to distract you from the shitty thing I did?

Anyway I was at dinner with some of these people and Spike mentioned working with Chris. I told him my story, and how five years had passed and I was still sitting on this feeling that I had blown it. Spike gently reminded me that it's never too late to reach out and apologize.

Spike told me he was looking at some similar themes in his new movie *Her*. What I didn't know then was how a year later I would watch that beautiful movie about loss and love with my wonderful new boyfriend, Nick Kroll. I would watch the scene where Joaquin Phoenix reads an apology letter he writes to his ex-wife, and I would cry for all the things behind me and all the things yet ahead. Spike offered to connect me to Marianne, and I gratefully agreed.

Then he sent me this:

From: Spike Jonze
Date: March 11, 2013
To: Amy Poehler
Subject: Fwd: Hey from Marianne & Chris

I didn't realize the whole situation.
I'll leave it in your hands.
I'm sorry, Amy.
Being a grown-up is hard.
Marianne is an awesome woman. I'm sure you guys
would get along great if you met in a different
situation.
big hugs
x

On March 11, 2013, Leone, Marianne wrote:

> **From:** Marianne Leone
> **Date:** March 11, 2013
> **To:** Spike Jonze
> **Subject:** Re: Hey from Marianne & Chris
>
> Yeah, I was furious at the skit she did on *SNL*
> and wrote her a letter to tell her. The skit was a
> gratuitously cruel slap at disability which wasn't
> funny in the least. What made it so, so horrible was
> that she was talking about the Somoza twins and
> the script I wrote about their lives. It was also the
> same night Hillary Clinton was on and I knew that

Anastasia was watching it with friends, since she was in Texas stumping for Hillary, so I knew she saw herself being parodied in a horrible, unfunny, cruel way. I was doubly insulted for the twins that Poehler never had the class to answer the letter, so, quite frankly, I am glad that it bothered her. (We had our return address on the letter, and, face it, we're not that hard to find.)

So, Spike, what I feel now is that I, we don't need an apology from her, but if she wants to make it up to ANASTASIA, she can contribute to her staying at London School of Economics for another year to get her Master's in Human Rights. Nothing will stop Anastasia. She will effect change in the world.

Love always,
Marianne

I read Marianne's e-mail and was devastated. I pictured Anastasia watching the show and seeing me make fun of her. I waited almost a month and sent this:

From: Amy Poehler
Date: April 1, 2013
To: Marianne Leone
Subject: Truly sorry

Dear Marianne and Chris,

I am writing to apologize. This is most likely an example of "too little too late" but I am writing to you to apologize for a Dakota Fanning sketch I did on *SNL* many years ago. It was a sketch that upset you and Anastasia, and one that moved you to write to me.

It has always bothered me that I never contacted you both. I regret that. I spoke of this to Spike and he very nicely connected us. I am grateful to him for giving me this opportunity, and appreciate you taking the time to read this.

I am very sorry for any pain I caused. I apologize for an insensitive portrayal of what was a loving and important project. I am truly sorry for hurting Anastasia in any way.

I do not think it's funny to make light of disabilities. This is not the kind of person I am or have ever been. The sketch was not written by me. The mean prop used was not seen by me until live on air. In fact,

I had no idea that we were referencing a real film.
I assumed it was yet another "adult" project that
we would joke about Dakota Fanning working on.
These are not excuses. I take responsibility for my
negligence in understanding the context of what
I was saying, but it's important for me to tell you
these details.

Anastasia deserves an apology from me. Feel free
to pass this along if you feel that is helpful or send
me her email if you deem it appropriate. I visited
her Indiegogo page. She is an awesome young woman
and I have no doubt she will continue to live an
amazing life.

Again, I am sorry. I send my best wishes to you and
your family, and my deepest condolences regarding
the loss of your son.

Thank you for reading this.
Amy.

Rereading it now I notice a few things. I got a little
caught up in the facts. I was hoping to defend myself.
But it felt really good to try. Apologies have nothing to
do with you. They are balloons in the sky. They may
never land. They may even choke a bird.
     Then I got this.

From: Anastasia Somoza
Date: April 7, 2013
To: Amy Poehler
Subject: Re: Fw: Truly sorry

Dear Amy,

Wow!!!! Oh my goodness, what a lovely surprise!!
Thank you so very much for your donation to my
campaign launched to raise funds that will hopefully
cover the cost of my caretakers in my 2nd year at LSE,
and for the kind message you wrote to Marianne and
Chris, which they graciously forwarded along to me.

They are two of the most amazingly wonderful, loving
people I know and have been incredible supporters
of me and my family!! I adore and admire them just as
much as I do my own parents, for countless reasons,
but most importantly for being a spectacular Mom
and Dad duo to gorgeous Jesse!! It is thanks to them,
Spike, many more of their closest friends and other
fabulous people that I am at LSE today stressing
out (like a typical grad student) over first year
final papers and comprehensive exams that are
fast approaching!

I always knew you never meant to hurt us in doing
the skit. After all, you didn't even know we actually
existed so I realized it wasn't personal. It also

certainly helps to know that you weren't aware
of the back story or real life references portrayed.
That being said, Chris, Marianne, my family and
I have worked tirelessly to make equal opportunity,
the inclusion and positive portrayal of people with
disabilities in society the norm rather than the
exception. As such, I was upset more generally
speaking, about the skit contributing to a severe
lack of knowledge, awareness, understanding and
empathy around disability. Too many people already
fear, and are often disgusted or put off in other
ways by disability and it saddened me to think of
the impact the skit may have had in adding fuel to
that fire.

Just as you felt relieved I'm sure, to have the
opportunity to apologize and express certain
details to Marianne, it is important to me that
you now know more about why the skit mattered.
I hope you understand that Marianne wrote to you
out of a deep love for her son, and my family for sure,
but also precisely because the struggle to change
the perception of disability goes far beyond us and
the more people exposed to this reality the better.

I've seen several episodes of your web series
Smart Girls at the Party and I truly believe that
the show's goal in celebrating "extraordinary
individuals who are changing the world by being

themselves," represents who you are and what you believe in, far more than the skit. It takes strength and character to admit responsibility by acknowledging, to Marianne and Chris, that you could and indeed should have done more to inform yourself about what you were being asked to act in the skit. I agree and greatly appreciate, admire and thank you for your honesty and willingness to recognize that.

The sincerity of your apology and your generosity mean more to me than you will ever know and it made my younger sister Gabriella giddy with excitement!!! I hope you're enjoying a sunny Sunday and thanks again from the bottom of my heart!!

Warmly,
Anastasia

Look at this woman. This beauty. What an act of grace. What a gift she gave me.

Shame makes people abandon their children and drink themselves to death. It also keeps us from true happiness. An apology is a glorious release. Anastasia gave me a huge gift. That e-mail changed me. It re-arranged my molecules. She has lived a life of struggle and decided not to pick up the armor. She teaches me about compassion. She makes her journey about open hearts. She is not ashamed.

Thankyouthankyouthankyou.

my books on
divorce

I UNDERSTAND WHY PEOPLE READ SO MANY BOOKS ON DIVORCE. When you are a person going through a divorce you feel incredibly alone, yet you are constantly reminded by society of how frequently divorce happens and how common it has become. You aren't allowed to feel special, but no one understands the specific ways you are in pain. Imagine spreading everything you care about on a blanket and then tossing the whole thing up in the air. The process of divorce is about loading up that blanket, throwing it up, watching it all spin, and worrying what stuff will break when it lands. It's no wonder we want to find answers and comfort.

I don't want to talk about my divorce because it is too sad and too personal. I also don't like people knowing my shit. I will say a few things. I am proud of how my ex-husband, Will, and I have been taking care of our children; I am beyond grateful he is their father; and I don't think a ten-year marriage constitutes failure.

That being said, getting a divorce really sucks. But as my dear friend and relationship sponsor Louis CK has noted, "divorce is always good news because no good marriage has ever ended in divorce."

Any painful experience makes you see things differently. It also reminds you of the simple truths that we purposely forget every day or else we would never get out of bed. Things like, nothing lasts forever and relationships can end. The best that can happen is you learn a little more about what you can handle and you stay soft through the pain. Perhaps you feel a little wiser. Maybe your experience can be of help to others. With that in mind, here are some titles for a series of divorce books I would like to pitch to you and my editors for future discussion. After review, I realize that all of my books have exclamation points at the end of their titles, but I think people want exclamation points in the titles of their books and I don't think I am wrong!!!!

1.

I WANT A DIVORCE!
SEE YOU TOMORROW!

If you have small children you will understand this book. This book deals with the fact that most people who divorce with small children still need to see each other every day. Any good parent will try to put their children's needs first, and so this book will help teach you how to have a knock-down, drag-out fight and still attend a kid's birthday party together on the same day. Are you in your early twenties and recently broke up with someone over Skype? This book is not for you. Have you successfully avoided your ex for over six months except for a close call at your friends' art opening? This book is not for you. Have you heard secondhand that your ex is building houses for Habitat for Humanity and you rolled your eyes at how fucking phony the whole thing sounded and then sighed because you don't miss him but you liked playing with his dog? This book is not for you. This book is for the people who have to work together or live together or co-parent together while going through a divorce.

Chapters include:
- FAKE SMILING
- HOW IMPORTANT IS THE LAST WORD?
- PHONE CALLS ON THE WAY HOME FROM THERAPY
- EVERYONE NEEDS TO STOP BUYING TOYS

2.

GET OVER IT! (BUT NOT TOO FAST!)

When you are going through the trauma and drama of divorce, you learn who your real friends are. They guide you and take care of you and save you from your darkest days. The problem is, you also have to talk to other people about this bullshit, and it's often people you don't care about or like. Usually these people are very interested at first and then have to go back to their own lives and want you to do the same. This book is here to remind you that even though you are in pain and still in transition, everyone else has moved on and is a little tired of your situation. This book will remind you that unless you and your ex-spouse got into a juicy fight or there are some new boyfriends and girlfriends in the mix, most people don't want to talk about it anymore. This book will also teach you how you need to move on, but not too fast. It will remind you that you are allowed to be upset, but for god's sake please keep it together. You need to seem sad at just the right times or else other people will think you're weird. You also need to be able to act normal at the parties they invite you to.

Chapters include:
- SHE DOESN'T CRY ENOUGH
- HE SEEMS GAY TO ME
- THIS WON'T GET YOU OUT OF A SPEEDING TICKET
- I'M SORRY TO INTERRUPT, BUT WHEN DO YOU THINK YOU WILL BE OVER IT?

3.

DIVORCE:
TEN WAYS TO NOT CATCH IT!

Divorce is contagious! Haven't you heard? It's like cancer but worse because no one really feels that bad for you. This book will teach you how to discuss your divorce with your currently married friends. Some married couples get freaked out when you talk about your divorce and like to tell you how they aren't going to get one. Usually they point to their hard work through therapy, their fear of being alone, or their total acceptance of a dead marriage devoid of sex and love. This book will help you not strangle them when they both stand in front of you and talk about how great their relationship continues to be. This book will also help you deal with the divorce voyeur, the friend who wants to hear every detail and live vicariously through your experience. This book will point to ways you can talk about your divorce without feeling like it's a fancy fur coat that people like to try on but then throw back at you in disgust because they would never wear something so vile. This book contains illustrations of happy couples looking at you with pity, and some weird aphorisms that intimate it's somehow easier to get divorced than to stay in an unhappy marriage.

Chapters include:

- DIVORCE IS NOT AN OPTION FOR ME,
  BUT I AM HAPPY FOR YOU
- C'MON, WHO HASN'T CHEATED?
- I JUST COULDN'T DO THAT TO MY KIDS
- MAYBE YOU GUYS JUST NEED TO GO TO
  OJAI FOR A WEEKEND

4.

HEY, LADY, I DON'T WANT TO FUCK YOUR HUSBAND!

Newly divorced and attending a wedding for the first time alone? This book is for you! Inside you will find ways to deal with the strange stares and drunk accusations that come along with not having a date. You will find tips on how to gently break it to women that you don't want to fuck their flabby baby-faced husbands. You will find pointers on how to deflect advances made by their husbands in full view of the wives so you don't have to get involved in other people's weird relationship shit. You will read about the experiences of other men and women who bravely attended events without a plus-one and came out alive. Check out our special section on what to do when friends try to awkwardly set you up, and our newly added bonus chapter dedicated to those who want to be gay for a weekend.

Chapters include:

- NO ONE AS GREAT AS YOU SHOULD BE SINGLE
- IS IT HARD TO BE AT A WEDDING?
- YOU'VE NEVER LOOKED BETTER
- HAVE YOU SEEN MARK ANYWHERE? I CAN'T FIND HIM

5.

GOD IS IN THE DETAILS!

This book will help you navigate all the intimate details that people want to know and, frankly, have a right to know. This includes how did you break up and where you are living now and who wanted it more and how long did you know and what is going on with the kids and how did you tell the kids and was it sad and is he mad and are you sad and does everyone know and who have you told and who can I tell and when will you make an announcement and does Margaret know and is it okay for me to call her and what's going on with the house and who is getting the money and how much money is it, exactly, and does Margaret know because I feel like she needs to hear it from me and do you have a boyfriend and does he have a girlfriend and what are their names and how much do they weigh and are weekends lonely and are you happier and do you think you will ever get married again and are you going to have more kids and could you just tell me exactly every detail from the beginning especially the bad stuff?

6.

THE HOLIDAYS ARE RUINED!

This book is one page long and just contains that one sentence. ———————

My hope is these manuals will help you navigate such a supremely shitty time. I promise you, someday happy couples won't make you cry anymore. Someday you may be in one again. Someday you will wake up feeling 51 percent happy and slowly, molecule by molecule, you will feel like yourself again. Or you will lose your mind and turn into a crazy person. Either way, let's just hope you avoided tattoos, because most are pretty stupid anyway.

talk to yourself
like you're ninety

I SUPPOSE I AM PRE-PERI-MIDDLE-AGED. At forty-three, I feel right in the middle. I am no spring chicken but I am not an old lady. I know the names of all the members of Odd Future but I didn't have the Internet in college. I can party like a twenty-year-old but it takes me almost a week to recover. Sometimes I am a tired mother taking her kids to the park, and other times I am a petulant teenager giving the finger to a speeding FedEx truck. I idle right in the middle.

I don't know when middle age starts, exactly. According to my current edition of the *Oxford English Dictionary*, middle age is "the period of life between young adulthood and old age, now usually regarded as between about forty-five and sixty." Sixty? Nice try, *Oxford*.

I think middle age begins once you start looking forward to eating dinner before six thirty, or when you call the cops when your next-door neighbor has a party. I know my body feels older. I recently hurt myself on a treadmill and it wasn't even on. I was adjusting my speed and stepped wrong and twisted my ankle. I felt a moment of frustration filled with immediate relief. I didn't have to actually work out, but I still got credit for trying. It was a gym snow day. You know those exercise pools where the water comes at you strong and you have to swim against it to build up your strength? That's what the social pressure of staying young feels like. You can either exhaust yourself thrashing against it or turn around and let the pressure of it massage out your kinks. Fighting aging is like the War on Drugs. It's expensive, does more harm than good, and has been proven to never end.

Hopefully I have another forty to fifty years of living ahead of me before I pass from this earth either in my sleep or during a daring rescue caught on tape. Ideally my penultimate day would be spent attending a giant beach party thrown in my honor. Everyone would gather around me at sunset, and the golden light would make my skin and hair beautiful as I told hilarious stories and gave away my extensive collection of moon art to my ex-lovers. I and all of my still-alive friends (which, let's face it, will mostly be women) would sing and dance late into the night. My sons would be grown and happy. I would be frail but adorable. I would still have my own teeth, and I would be tended to by handsome and kind gay men who pruned me like a bonsai tree. Once the party ended, everyone would fall asleep except for me. I would spend the rest of the night watching the stars under a nice blanket my grand-daughter made with her Knit-Bot 5000. As the sun began to rise, an unexpected guest would wake and put the coffee on. My last words would be something banal and beautiful. "Are you warm enough?" my guest would ask. "Just right," I would answer. My funeral would be huge but incredibly intimate. I would instruct people to throw firecrackers on my funeral pyre and play *Purple Rain* on a loop.

It wasn't until I turned thirty that I started to feel like my adult life was beginning. I had just been hired on *Saturday Night Live* and was about to attend my own surprise dance party; then September 11 came and the whole world went bananas. I had met Will and I knew I wanted to marry him and try to have children someday. I had paid off my student loans and I knew how to jump-start my own car battery. I had spent so much of my twenties in a state of delayed adolescence and so much of my teenage years wishing and praying that time would move faster. I remembered being five years old when my mother turned thirty. My dad threw a big party for her and the adults got drunk in the base-ment. I sat on the stairs in Holly Hobbie pajamas and listened to the clinking sound of ice in glasses. They all brought dirty presents from Spencer Gifts, a joke shop in our local mall that had boob mugs and fart machines and penis pasta. We would go in there as kids and

sneak peeks at the dirty stuff, pretending to understand the bad sex jokes. Ten years later, for my mom's
fortieth, my dad made a homemade "Buns" calendar
that included relatives and friends. They all posed in
various funny underwear. Some were in Speedos playing the piano and others were in saggy pants showing
their butt crack while fixing the kitchen sink. All this
was the kind of groovy, semi-lewd suburban stuff that
in some instances led to "key parties." Thankfully, at
least to my knowledge, there was no wife swapping in
my childhood home. If there was, I don't want to know
about it. Family, please remember this when you all
write your inevitable and scathing memoirs.

At thirty I felt like I had about six or seven years of
feeling like a real adult before my brain and society
started to make me worry about being old. There is the
built-in baby stuff, plus the added fascination with the
new. But here's the thing. Getting older is awesome, and
not because you don't care as much about what people
think. It's awesome because you develop secret super-
powers. Behold:

Getting older makes you somewhat invisible. This
can be exciting. Now that you are better at observing a
situation, you can use your sharpened skills to scan a
room and navigate it before anyone even notices you
are there. This can lead to your finding a comfortable
couch at a party, or to the realization that you are at a
terrible party and need to leave immediately. Knowing
when to exit is a great aspect of being older, and since

you are invisible, no one will even notice you are gone. Not getting immediate attention can mean you decide how and when you want people to look at you. Remember all those goofy comedies in the eighties where men became invisible and hung out in women's locker rooms? Remember how the men got to watch pretty girls take showers and snap each other with towels? You can do this, but in a different way. You can witness young people embarrassing themselves and get a thrill that it's not you. You can watch them throw around their "alwayses" and "nevers" and "I'm the kind of person who's" and delight in the fact that you are past that point in your life. Feeling invisible means you can float. You can decide to travel without permission. You know secrets and hear opinions that weren't meant for you to hear. Plus, it's easier to steal things.

Getting older also helps you develop X-ray vision. The strange thing is that the moment people start looking at you less is when you start being able to see through people more. You get better at understanding what people mean and how it can be different from what they say. Finally the phrase "actions speak louder than words" starts to make sense. You can read people's energies better, and this hopefully means you get stuck talking to less duds. You also may start to seek out duds, as some kind of weird emotional exercise to test your boundaries. You use the word "boundaries." You can witness bad behavior and watch it like you would watch someone else's child having a tantrum. Gone are the days (hopefully) when you take everything personally and internalize everyone's behavior. You get better at knowing what you want and need. You can tell what kind of underwear people are wearing.

Lastly, because you are a superhero, you are really good at putting together a good team. You can look around the room and notice the other superheroes because they are the ones noticing you. The friends you meet over forty are really juicy. They are highly emulsified and full of flavor. Now that you're starting to have a sense of who you are, you know better what kind of friend you want and need. My peers are crushing it right now and it's totally amazing and energizing to watch. I have made friends with older women whom I have admired for years who let me learn from their experience. I drink from their life well. They tell me about hormones and vacation spots and neck cream. I am interested in people who swim in the deep end. I want to have conversations about real things with people who have experienced real things. I'm tired of talking about movies and gossiping about friends. Life is crunchy and complicated and all the more delicious.

Now that I am older, I am rounder and softer, which isn't always a bad thing. I remember fewer names so I try to focus on someone's eyes instead. Sex is better and I'm better at it. I don't miss the frustration of youth, the anticipation of love and pain, the paralysis of choices still ahead. The pressure of "What are you going to do?" makes everybody feel like they haven't done anything yet. Young people can remind us to take chances and be angry and stop our patterns. Old people can remind us to laugh more and get focused and make friends with our patterns. Young and old need to relax in the moment and live where they are. Be Here Now, like the great book says.

I have work to do. I remain suspicious of men and women who don't want to work with their peers, comedy writers who only hire newbies, and people who only date someone younger or of lower status. Don't you want the tree you love or work with to have a similar number of rings? Sometimes I get scared that I have missed out or checked out. Occasionally I don't recognize myself in a store window. When this happens, I try to speak to myself from the future. This is possible since time travel is real and I have the proof (more on this later). Here's what my ninety-year-old self tells me:

✳ Get to the point, please.

✳ Talk slower and louder.

✳ You look great and you are beautiful.

✳ Can you walk? Stop complaining.

✳ Stopcomplainingstopcomplainingstopcomplaining.

✳ Stop whining about getting old. It's a privilege.
A lot of people who are dead wish they were still alive.

✳ Ignore what other people think. Most people aren't
even paying attention to you.

✳ Find a nice boy who is nice to you.

✳ Isn't dancing fun?

✳ Let's not talk about people dying.

✳ Don't go too long without talking to your family.

✳ Forgive your parents for what they never gave you.

✳ Eat some nice soup and you will feel better.
Or take a walk.

✳ Relax and let her win. Who cares?

✳ Whocareswhocareswhocareswhocareswhocares?

✳ Make "No" a complete sentence.

✳ Kiss every baby and pet every dog.

✳ Walk slowly and lie down when you're tired.

✳ What's next?

✳ That next-door neighbor is too loud; that's it,
I'm calling the cops.